When God asks for EVERYTHING

Dorothea Mokgadi

Published by Bethel Publishing House, 2025.

While every precaution has been taken in the preparation of this book, the publisher assumes no responsibility for errors or omissions, or for damages resulting from the use of the information contained herein.

WHEN GOD ASKS FOR EVERYTHING

First edition. November 19, 2025.

ISBN: 978-1037098048

Written by Dorothea Mokgadi.

Dedication

Dedication

To God, the Source of all wisdom, fire, and glory, who calls us beyond comfort into the fullness of His life.To the seekers, the broken, and the faithful who dare to surrender everything to follow Him, may your journey of yielding become your greatest worship.

To the One who asked for everything... and gave me everything in return. To **Jesus Christ**, my Lord, my Master, my Eternal Bridegroom, this book is Your inheritance in me. You walked me through the Cross, the Fire, and into the Glory. Every word written here is born of surrender, tears, obedience, and the weight of Your Presence. To the **Holy Spirit**, my Comforter, my teacher, and closest Friend, thank You for brooding over every chapter, just as You brooded over the waters at creation. You birthed this book through groanings too deep for words.

To **Abba Father**, who never gave up on His daughter, who whispered identity to me even when I was lost in the fire, this is my eternal "yes" to Your plan.

And to the **nations still waiting,** especially China and South Africa, this book is for you. I was sent ahead with a message: *The Bridegroom is coming. Trim your lamps. Prepare the way of the Lord.*

Epigraphy

"When He asks for everything, it is not to take from you, but to give you Himself. In surrender, the soul discovers its true glory." -Prophetess Dorothea Telephone Mokgadi

Wʜᴇɴ ɢᴏᴅ ᴀsᴋs ғᴏʀ EVERYTHING

THE CROSS, THE FIRE, AND THE GLORY
DOROTHEA TELEPHONE MOKGADI

Wʜᴇɴ ɢᴏᴅ ᴀsᴋs ғᴏʀ EVERYTHING

THE CROSS, THE FIRE, AND THE GLORY
DOROTHEA TELEPHONE MOKGADI

Author: Prophetess Dorothea Telephone Mokgadi
Publisher: Bethel Publishing House
ISBN: 978-1-03-709804-8
Contact:
Phone: +27 72 972 9866
Email: mokgadidorothy6@gmail.com
Edited by: Patience Sakutukwa
Proofread by: Bethel Publishing House
Formatting & Typesetting: Bethel Publishing House
Cover Design: Bethel Publishing House
Printing: Bethel Publishing House

Epigraphy

"When He asks for everything, it is not to take from you, but to give you Himself.
In surrender, the soul discovers its true glory." -Prophetess Dorothea Telephone
Mokgadi

Dedication

To God the Source of all wisdom, fire, and glory who calls us beyond comfort into the fullness of His life.

To the seekers, the broken, and the faithful who dare to surrender everything to follow Him may your journey of yielding become your greatest worship.

To the One who asked for everything... and gave me everything in return. To **Jesus Christ**, my Lord, my Master, my Eternal Bridegroom this book is Your inheritance in me. You walked me through the Cross, the Fire, and into the Glory. Every word written here is born of surrender, tears, obedience, and the weight of Your Presence. To the **Holy Spirit**, my Comforter, my teacher, and closest Friend thank You for brooding over every chapter, just as You brooded over the waters at creation. You birthed this book through groanings too deep for words.

To **Abba Father**, who never gave up on His daughter, who whispered identity to me even when I was lost in the fire this is my eternal "yes" to Your plan.

And to the **nations still waiting** especially China and South Africa this book is for you. I was sent ahead with a message: *The Bridegroom is coming. Trim your lamps. Prepare the way of the Lord.*

Acknowledgements

I acknowledge the sovereign hand of Almighty God Yahweh, The Eternal One, the Source of all life and destiny. You called me before I was formed, whispered nations into my spirit, and authored my journey with holy fire. Thank You, Father, for trusting me with revelation, for walking with me through silence and storm, for speaking when I needed answers, and for staying near when I did not know how to ask. Holy Spirit, my Counsellor and Oil of Understanding you are my daily strength. And to my Beloved Jesus Christ my Bridegroom, my Intercessor, and my Coming King I live to tell Your story. I honour **Dr. L.E.D. Pika**, my Bishop, mentor, and the visionary of World Harvest Theological College, whose unwavering teachings laid a firm foundation for my walk with God. To all my lecturers **Pastor Bheki Maseko, Pastor Titcha, Pastor Moses Kabanje, Pastor Jacob, and Pastor Refiloe** thank you for your faithfulness and for shaping my understanding of truth. To **my sons and my mother**, who stood beside me when hope seemed lost your love gave me the strength to rise again.

To **Lorraine Mdluli**, thank you for speaking life when I could not find breath. **Hilda Mathe**, my dearest friend your steadfast encouragement became a pillar in this journey. **Vinolia Mathipa**, thank you for keeping the midnight oil burning with me in intercession. And to all who have believed in the calling upon my life even in silence this is your fruit, too. May this book stand as a testimony, not only of my obedience, but of **God's unfailing faithfulness**.

Foreword

Have you ever felt the gentle tug of God on your heart, so persistent that you cannot ignore it? Or the sudden stillness in a moment of chaos, when it seems the heavens, themselves are leaning in to speak? *When God Asks for Everything: The Cross, the Fire, and the Glory* is born from such moments where the ordinary brushes against the extraordinary, and where surrender becomes not a choice, but a necessity. Prophetess Dorothea Telephone Mokgadi invites you into her world a world of brokenness, fire, and resurrection. Through her experiences, we see that God's ways are often mysterious, sometimes painful, yet always purposeful. This book does not merely recount events; it brings you into the heartbeat of those encounters, allowing you to feel the silence of waiting, the refining heat of trials, and the breathtaking revelation of His glory.

As you journey through these pages, you will:

1. **Walk a Journey of Surrender:** Encounter moments where letting go is the only way forward.
2. **Be Refined Through Fire:** Discover that trials are not punishment but preparation for greater purpose.
3. **See His Glory Revealed:** Witness how brokenness can become a vessel for divine light.
4. **Grow in Intimacy with God:** Learn to hear His voice and know Him beyond routine and ritual.
5. **Receive Healing and Wholeness:** Find hope in your wilderness, knowing it shapes you for destiny.
6. **Answer the Call to Live Set Apart:** Be challenged to align your life fully with God's will and timing.

This is a book to be savoured, not rushed. Each chapter, each reflection, and each prayer is an invitation to step closer to God's heart.

Mmbulaheni Mashudu Worship
Author & Motivational Speaker

Preface

There comes a moment in every believer's life when God asks for everything. Not part of your heart, not just your talents, but your comfort, your dreams, your very self. I know this moment well. Through seasons of breaking, refining, and fire, I have been confronted with God's call to total surrender, and I have learned that it is in giving Him all that we receive everything.

When God Asks for Everything: The Cross, the Fire, and the Glory is the outpouring of my reflections, encounters, and revelations during those seasons. This is not a manual to follow, nor a distant testimony to admire it is an invitation. An invitation for you to journey with me through the refining fires, the silence, the pain, and the revelation of God's glory.

Throughout these pages, you will find scripture reflections, journal prompts, and prayers designed to help you not only read, but experience the presence and heartbeat of God. My prayer is that as you navigate these chapters, you will be challenged, comforted, and inspired to surrender fully and in doing so, discover that the Cross is not the end, the fire is not destruction, and surrender is not loss, but the doorway to resurrection power and unshakable glory.

Introduction

What happens when God asks for everything your comfort, your dreams, your relationships, even your very identity? I have asked myself this question many times. And through the seasons of my own life, I have discovered that His call is never easy, but it is always perfect. This book is my journey my encounters with God, the nights of desperate prayer, the heavenly visitations, the moments of fire, and the glimpses of glory. I am sharing these experiences not to tell you what to do, but to walk with you through the reality of surrender, breaking, and divine transformation. As you read, I invite you to come with an open heart and a willing spirit. You will not only read words you will experience what it means to wait in silence, to trust when everything seems lost, and to be refined in the fire of God's purpose.

Within these pages, you will find reflections, scripture, journal prompts, and prayers tools to help you encounter God more deeply. My hope is that as you journey through this book, surrender will no longer feel like loss, but like the pathway to glory. When God asks for everything, it is only because He desires to give you Himself and that is the greatest gift you can ever receive. Are you ready to step into what God is asking of you, to lay down all for Him, and to receive the life He has prepared beyond your surrender?

PART I

THE CALL & AWAKENING

Chapter 1

A Child of the Wind

"Before I formed you in the womb, I knew you, and before you were born, I set you apart; I appointed you as a prophet to the nations." – Jeremiah 1:5

I was born in 1971, in a small village called Legonyane in the Northwest, South Africa. We had no riches, no title, and no great reputation. But something was planted in me from the very beginning a hunger for the voice of God. From the early age of five, I would be caught in deep conversation not with myself, but with God. My mother would beat me, not out of cruelty, but out of confusion. She could not see the One I was speaking to, but I heard Him clearly. I was a child of the wind, blown by visions, whispers, and impressions I could never escape.

While other children played, I wandered alone, thinking, asking, and listening. I didn't crave company; I longed for answers. At thirteen, during confirmation in the Lutheran Church, I attended an evangelical tent meeting in our village. The preacher called for those who wanted to receive Jesus. I walked to the front. The next day, the priest at the Lutheran Church asked me, "Did you receive Christ?" I said, "Yes." He took a shambok (whip) and said, "Then I must beat that Christ out of you." I was confused. I asked God, "Do all these churches have different Jesuses?" I was only a child, but I already knew God was not confused men were.

A Life Set Apart

My grandmother was a prayerful woman who heard the voice of God audibly. She saw something in me and told my family, *"Listen to her when she speaks. What she sees, it happens."* They didn't always believe me, but I kept seeing. Kept dreaming.

Kept hearing. As I grew, I was often sick, and no doctor could explain it. They took me to a traditional healer, who said, *"This child is not for traditional medicine. She is different. She is for prayer. Only prayer will heal her."*

The Mark of the Intercessor

Everywhere I went, people called me a woman of prayer. Even before I could fully understand it, the altar was forming in me. The fire was growing. I was being marked for intercession not by the laying on of hands, but by the unseen hand of God.

Teaching

Recognizing the Call

God often plants the seed of calling long before we understand it. Jeremiah 1:5 reminds us that God's purpose is not an afterthought; it is embedded in our very design.

Many are called from the womb, and like Samuel or Jeremiah, the signs begin early. Dreams, deep questions, strange spiritual awareness, or an unexplainable desire to be alone with God can be early indicators. When you're a child of the Wind, the Holy Spirit begins moving before you can explain what's happening. Your spirit recognizes a realm your mind has not yet been taught. You may feel pulled aside, even rejected by others not because something is wrong with you, but because something is right with your purpose.

Spiritual Misunderstanding

Being misunderstood by family, the church, or culture does not disqualify you; it often marks you. Rejection, ridicule, or resistance can be evidence of divine distinction. When the Lutheran priest rejected me for receiving Christ, I learned a vital truth: man's religion cannot define God's relationship.

God's call creates separation. It draws you into a wilderness others cannot understand. It forms an altar within you, a place of encounter, prayer, vision, and fire. When God marks you as an intercessor or prophetic voice, your life becomes a tabernacle a meeting place where the wind speaks and the fire falls.

You Were Born for the Wind

The Wind is the Spirit. To be a child of the Wind means to live a life blown by His direction, invisible yet unstoppable. You will not fit into normal molds. You will not be comfortable in shallow religion. You will ache for depth, for truth, and for a face-to-face walk with God. Your hunger is proof of your assignment.

Reflections

Have you ever felt misunderstood for your spiritual hunger?

- Are there moments in your childhood that now make sense in the light of your calling?
- What winds of the Spirit were already blowing before anyone else noticed?
- Can you remember a time when the altar of prayer began forming in your heart?
- Who were the voices (like your grandmother) that affirmed you are calling even before you understood it?

Journal Prompt

Write a letter to your younger self. Remind her that the strange, lonely feelings, the visions, and the questions were not signs of being broken they were signs of being called. Speak prophetically over her life. Affirm what God already knew.

Prayer

Father, you knew me before I was formed. You appointed me before the world approved me. You called me when I could not yet speak, and You walked with me when others walked away. Thank You for marking me. Thank You for the hunger. Thank You for the wind. Let me never silence the voice I heard as a child. Let me never trade the altar for applause. Let me never lose the wonder of hearing You. Raise up many who are children of the Wind. Let them know they are not alone. Let the misunderstood find meaning. Let the called find courage. In Jesus' name, Amen.

Chapter 2

The Night God Asked for Everything

"Offer your bodies as a living sacrifice, holy and acceptable to God, this is your spiritual act of worship." – Romans 12:1

It was the year 2002. The house was still. My husband wasn't home. My two little children were asleep. I knelt on the floor in the middle of the night, tears streaming down my face. I was not just praying; I was weeping from a place I could not explain. My heart was broken. I was a widow in a living marriage unseen, unheard, unloved. And I cried out: *"Lord, when will the pain stop? When will I be free from this silence and sorrow?"* That night, Heaven broke through.

The Voice That Called Me Deeper

As I knelt, I heard His voice clear, holy, and unwavering: *"Surrender your whole life to Me."* I was led in a prayer I did not create.

My spirit followed every word that came, not from my thoughts, but from the mouth of God. This was not a casual rededication; it was total surrender. God was not asking for more time He was asking for everything: my comfort, my reputation, my control, my husband, my dreams, my very self.

A New Fire Began

The next day, I felt a stirring in my spirit to find a Spirit-filled church. I obeyed. That Sunday, a visiting apostle preached and called for those ready to surrender. I hesitated, but before I knew it, I was already standing at the front, arms lifted, tears flowing. As he moved to lay hands on us, something extraordinary happened. When he reached me, he suddenly fell backwards. Stunned, he said publicly: *"The power in you is strong."* I was overwhelmed. This was the first time someone saw what me had always been inside. God was activating what He had already anointed.

The Cost of Obedience

That night marked the beginning of a pattern of loss. Little by little, everything I leaned on began to fall away. I lost possessions. Relationships shifted. Even my marriage eventually ended. But something deeper was happening. God was stripping me to clothe me in glory. He was taking away the "me" so He could reveal Christ in me.

Teaching

Romans 12:1 is not a light invitation; it is a radical call to worship through total surrender. Worship is not only in the songs we sing but in the sacrifices we offer. True worship costs something. In this chapter, the Lord called for everything comfort, identity, even the sacred parts of life we try to protect. When God asks for everything, He is not being cruel. He is preparing to pour in everything of Himself. This kind of surrender opens the door for transformation.

We are no longer conformed to the pattern of this world but renewed in our minds to know His will (Romans 12:2). The pain you experience in surrender is never wasted; it becomes the soil where divine purpose takes root.

Reflections

Have you ever had a night where God asked you for everything?

1. What fears rise when you realize that surrender includes loss?
2. What did God begin to build in you after everything was stripped away?

Journal Prompt

Write about a time when God asked you to surrender something deeply personal. What was your immediate reaction? What did He reveal about Himself through your obedience?

Prayer

Lord, I come before You with trembling hands and an open heart. I do not understand all You ask of me, but I trust Your love. If You are asking for everything, it is because You want to fill me with all that You are. I lay down my life, my fears, and my plans. Take all me and build something eternal with my surrender. In Jesus' name, Amen.

Chapter 3

17

The Crown of Thorns

"He was despised and rejected by men, a Man of sorrows and acquainted with grief... and by His wounds we are healed." – Isaiah 53:3, 5

Between 2004 and 2015, I had just returned from a prayer walk, my usual custom walking the streets at night, speaking to God while everyone else slept. The pain in my marriage had grown unbearable. Events in my life felt like a river I could not stop. I was constantly crying, asking God: *"Why this suffering? Why this silence?"* A few days earlier, my friend and I had been reading the Bible line by line, birthing a women's ministry in my home. That morning, before dawn, after hours of prayer, she looked at me and said: *"There is something God wants to say to you."* Then she left. I lay prostrate on the floor, alone.

The Instruction that Pierced Me

Around 4:00 a.m., I heard His voice: *"Remove your husband from where you've placed him in your heart. Put Me there. I will find the place where he fits in your life."* I struggled to obey. My heart was torn between love and obedience. But I knew this was holy confrontation. God was not asking for more room He was demanding His throne.

The Night Christ Entered My Bedroom

Later that year, in 2015, everything changed. I had just finished another street prayer walk and sat by the pool to pray. As I stepped into my bedroom, the room was covered in a pure white cloud. Then I saw Him. Christ appeared in my room, wearing a crown of thorns. His face was bloody. Tears flowed from His eye's tears of blood. He looked at me with sorrow deeper than words and asked: *"Was My death in vain for you?"*

The Question that Wounded & Healed

Those words cut like a sword. I fell into sobs. I couldn't answer, because I knew. He wasn't just asking me; He was revealing my heart. That night I realized I had wanted Him as Saviour, but I had not fully embraced Him as Lord. I wanted rescue, but He was calling me to resurrection. And resurrection always requires a death. Since that night, the memory has never left me. The image of Christ, bleeding, weeping, asking, became a permanent engraving in my soul. It was no longer just about ministry; it became about Him His suffering, His love, His ownership over my life.

Teaching

In this sacred chapter, we encounter the essence of surrender. Christ is not only the One who saves us from sin, but the Lord who must reign in our hearts.

The moment He asked, *"Was My death in vain for you?"* reveals His desire to not be a visitor in our lives, but the Owner of our hearts. Many believers embrace the cross for its benefits peace, healing, protection but shy away from the surrender it demands. True resurrection life only flows from crucified flesh. That question is not condemnation; it is invitation an invitation into a deeper walk with Him, where every idol must fall, even the ones we love. The crown of thorns upon His head speaks of the suffering He endured for our minds to be renewed. The tears of blood reveal His longing for intimacy with us. His pain was emotional, spiritual, and deeply personal. Christ's appearing was not to rebuke, but to awaken. He was reminding us that nothing and no one can occupy the throne that belongs to Him alone.

Journal Prompt

Sit in silence before God. Ask Him to reveal if there is anything or anyone seated on the throne of your heart in His place. Write your honest response to this question: *"Lord, was Your death in vain in this area of my life?"* Let Him speak. Let Him heal.

Reflections

1. What have you placed on the throne that belongs to Christ alone?
2. How would you answer Him if He asked you, *"Was My death in vain for you?"*
3. What moment in your life permanently marked your faith journey?

DOROTHEA MOKGADI

Prayer

Lord Jesus, I come before You humbled and undone. Forgive me for placing anything or anyone in the place that belongs to You alone. I remember Your crown of thorns, your tears of blood, and the question that broke me: *"Was My death in vain?"* Today I say no Your death was not in vain, not in my life, not in my story. Take Your place again. Rule in my heart. Be both Saviour and Lord. I surrender my idols, my fears, my loves, and my future to You. Let Your suffering not be wasted in me. Amen.

Chapter 4

The House Covered in Fire

"For He will command His angels concerning you to guard you in all your ways... His faithfulness will be your shield and rampart." – Psalm 91:11, 4

Not long after Christ appeared to me, a different type of confrontation came. This time, it wasn't an inner battle; it was warfare from the enemy himself

The Dragon and the Fire

One night, as we were sleeping, I had a vision. In it, Satan stood before me and said: *"I will kill you before you deliver the people God has called you for."* He meant it; I could feel the rage.

The fire began rushing toward my home, where my husband and children lay asleep. Just when the flames were about to consume us, a purple silk cloth, like royalty, descended from Heaven and gently fell over my house and yard. The fire could not enter. The flames had no power. I turned to the enemy and declared: *"Jesus has the power, not you."*

A Real Fire in the Natural

The vision ended, but suddenly, we woke up to the smell of smoke. Our physical house was filled with it. My husband jumped up and ran to the DB board (electrical unit) and shut everything down. There had been an electrical surge. What I saw in the spirit had tried to manifest in the natural, but it could not succeed.

The Dwelling Place of Glory

The purple cloth was not just protection; it was a mantle of consecration. God had marked our home. From that time on, strange things began to happen:

- People came to my house and were instantly healed.
- Some entered and began crying without knowing why.
- Others said they felt fire and peace at the same time.
- One man came to the house and said, *"I saw fire surrounding your house as I passed by."*

Witches were uncomfortable. The broken found comfort. The sick was healed without any prayer. It wasn't me. It was the Presence that had settled.

A House of Apostolic Fire

This was no longer just a house. It had become a dwelling of glory, an altar of healing, a gateway of deliverance a place of fire. God had chosen the humble home of a woman who had lost everything to reveal His unshakable presence.

Teaching

The vision and events surrounding the purple cloth reveal the reality of spiritual warfare and divine protection. God marks places and people for His glory, and when He does, no force in hell can penetrate that divine seal. The purple cloth symbolizes royal covering, God's authority, consecration, and presence. In Scripture, purple often represented kingship and sacredness (see Exodus 26:1; Mark 15:17). When this cloth descended upon the house, it was as if Heaven itself declared: *"This dwelling belongs to Me."*

Every believer is called to create dwelling places of God's glory not just churches, but homes, hearts, and even regions. This chapter invites us to take seriously the atmosphere of our homes and lives. God is still choosing ordinary places to manifest His extraordinary presence.

As in the Psalm, God commands His angels to protect us not just for safety, but so that His purposes in our lives can be fulfilled. Just as the enemy threatened Dorothy's calling, many of us face threats and opposition that are about the destiny we carry. But take courage: the fire cannot enter when Heaven has sealed your home.

Reflections

1. Has God ever marked a place in your life as holy?
2. In what ways has the enemy tried to destroy what God was birthing in you?
3. What would it look like to consecrate your home as an altar of glory?

Prayer

Father, thank You for being the shield around me and my family. Thank You for the fire of Your presence that protects, heals, and delivers. I dedicate my home to You let it be a place where Heaven touches earth, a dwelling place for Your glory. Cover us in the purple cloth of Your royal grace. Let every scheme of the enemy be turned back by the fire of Your love. In Jesus' name, Amen.

Chapter 5

Healing Hands & the Oil

"You anoint my head with oil; my cup overflows." – Psalm 23:5

It was not during a conference. Not under the lights of a church. Not even with a preacher present. This encounter happened in a place of remembrance the ground of my grandmother's home. The place where the prophetic journey was first observed and where the Spirit chose to visit again.

Digging in the Ground of Legacy

In a vision, I found myself kneeling and praying at my granny's place. My hands were in the soil, digging. But I wasn't planting or searching for something. Suddenly, from the ground came pure oil. It began to flow through my fingers not thick or dark, but pure and clean.

The oil was alive. I could feel the weight of Heaven in it. And then I heard the Lord say: *"Do not defile your hands. These are healing hands."*

The Anointing You Didn't Ask For

From that moment, I noticed that when I touched people in obedience, healing would come. Deliverance would happen. Prophetic insight would flow like water. I had never asked for the gift of healing, but the oil had chosen me. God had ordained that my hands carry His virtue not just for ministry, but for those He sent across my path, even in ordinary places.

A Life of Consecration

But with that oil came a holy warning:

"Do not defile your hands." These were not hands to entertain sin. Not hands to be laid on just anyone. Not hands to be entangled in romantic defilement. The Lord reminded me again:

"Keep your body holy for My use."

And for seven years after my divorce, I have honoured that vow not by law, but by love. Because once you've felt oil drip from Heaven, you don't sell your hands for empty comfort.

Healing Flows in Obedience

Healing is not always loud. Sometimes it flows in silence through a hug, through prayer, through your very presence. God said to me:

"You are an instrument of quiet deliverance."

Teaching

The anointing of healing is not always given with loud declarations or dramatic ceremonies. Sometimes, it is birthed in the soil of remembrance in places were God first planted legacy. The vision of oil flowing from the ground at my grandmother's home is not just symbolic; it is deeply spiritual.

It reveals how healing anointing often comes through generational faithfulness and the honouring of one's roots. In the Bible, oil signifies consecration, healing, and divine enablement. When God declares that a person has *"healing hands,"* it is a call to be set apart an invitation to walk in purity, obedience, and deep sensitivity to the Holy Spirit. Healing ministry is sacred and must be stewarded with reverence, not flaunted or commercialised. We learn that healing flows through obedience, not performance.

It doesn't always manifest with visible miracles, but sometimes through presence, touch, and love. The consecration of hands and body is critical. Holiness is not legalism; it is the fragrance of love returned to the One who poured the oil. Like the psalmist, when God anoints your head with oil, your cup will overflow into others' lives.

Reflections

1. Has God ever asked you to consecrate a part of your body for His glory?
2. Are there gifts in your life that you didn't ask for but were entrusted with?
3. How are you protecting the oil He has poured over your life?

Journal Prompt

Spend time reflecting on the places where God first encountered you or gave you specific instructions. Write a letter to God, recommitting your hands, your

DOROTHEA MOKGADI

service, your touch, and your creativity to His purpose. Ask the Holy Spirit to help you protect the healing oil entrusted to you.

Prayer

Father, thank You for the oil of healing that flows not by might nor by power, but by Your Spirit. Thank You for choosing my hands to carry Your virtue. Help me to walk in purity, in obedience, and in quiet faithfulness. Teach me how to love as You love, to touch as You touch, and to serve as You served. May the oil on my life never be defiled. In Jesus' name, Amen.

PART II

THE CROSS &GETHSEMANE

Chapter 6

The Crushing: Process

It was in 2021, shortly after an all-night prayer meeting. The Spirit of the Lord had moved in power, and our hearts were stirred with hunger. That early morning, I returned home and laid down to rest. I had prayed, and I felt peace as I drifted into sleep. As I slept, something extraordinary began to happen my feet caught fire. The fire was not natural but spiritual. It was alive, vibrant, and holy. I could see the flames clearly orange and gold burning with divine intensity yet not consuming. It was a fire from Heaven. Then I heard the unmistakable voice of God not a whisper of imagination, but a thunder in my spirit that shook me to the core:

"I have anointed you as an Apostle."

The fire burned stronger with those words. I knew this was not a dream; it was an ordination from the Throne Room itself. From that day forward, the fire in my feet has never left me. It has walked with me through valleys, nations, visions, and assignments. Many servants of God have confirmed this calling in my life without knowing the details. But I know what I saw. I know what I heard. And I know what I carry. This was not man's doing. It was God's choosing.

Teaching

The Apostolic Fire

In the Scriptures, fire often symbolizes God's presence, purification, commissioning, and power. From Moses at the burning bush (Exodus 3) to the tongues of fire at Pentecost (Acts 2), God uses fire to signify divine encounters and new assignments. The feet are symbolic of movement, territory, and apostolic mission. In Ephesians 6:15, Paul writes:

"And having shod your feet with the preparation of the gospel of peace..." And again, in Isaiah 52:7: *"How beautiful upon the mountains are the feet of him who brings good news..."* When your feet are on fire, Heaven is declaring: "You are being sent." The flames mean more than zeal they mean divine propulsion. God

is placing His fire where your obedience will carry you. It is not for standing still.

It is to go, with authority, healing, and message. The call to apostleship is not glamorous. It is a call to suffering, foundation-laying, and going where others dare not go. Paul said in 1 Corinthians 4:9: *"For it seems to me that God has put us apostles on display at the end of the procession, like those condemned to die..."* To be an apostle is to carry burdens that birth regions into revival and to war in realms unseen. The fire in your feet is not just a feeling it is an activation.

Reflections

- Have you ever sensed God preparing you for something greater even before others could see it?
- Have your feet ever burned spiritually with the urgency to go, preach, or obey?
- Are you willing to walk where few will go even if it costs you?

The apostolic fire is not about title; it is about being sent. Many are called, but few are set ablaze.

Journal Prompt

- Describe a time you felt an invisible fire urging you to move in obedience.
- What has God spoken to you about your calling something perhaps only Heaven has confirmed?
- Write a letter to God, responding to His voice: *"I have anointed you..."*

Prayer

Lord Jesus, I surrender my feet to Your fire. Burn away hesitation. Burn away fear. Let my life carry Your message with purity, obedience, and courage. Thank You for setting me apart, not by man's oil, but by Heaven's flame. Wherever You send me, I will go. Wherever my feet tread, may the Gospel leave footprints of glory. May I never walk without Your presence again. Set my feet on fire for Your Kingdom. In Jesus' Name, Amen.

Chapter 7

Actress In the Story of God

There are moments when Heaven speaks so softly, yet so clearly, that the earth must pause to listen. One such moment came in an unexpected way through something as simple as a Chinese drama. Late in 2021, I found myself drawn to stories from a distant land not just entertained but captivated. I began watching Chinese dramas, learning the language, and even preparing traditional dishes with curiosity and joy. What started as a simple interest soon revealed itself to be a divine setup. It was not culture I was chasing but calling. One evening, the Lord whispered to me: *"I will send you there for the work of ministry."*

My heart stood still. Everything made sense in an instant. I was not watching someone else's story unfold on a screen; I was being written into a greater one. And though I have never physically set foot in China, I have walked its soil many times in the Spirit through recurring visions, dreams, and supernatural visitations. I knew I was being prepared for something eternal. Later, the voice of the Lord came again:

"You enjoy watching other people's movies and stories. Now, I will make you an actress in the story I, the Lord, have written."

Living the Script of Heaven

At first, I didn't fully understand what He meant. But slowly, the Holy Spirit unfolded the revelation in my heart. I realized I was not just a spectator of destiny. I was not a background character in life's drama.

I had been handpicked not for a role in a man's performance, but for a holy scene in God's unfolding story. I wasn't just called. I was cast by the Master Director. I wasn't merely chosen. I was positioned to carry His glory to the nations including those I had only walked in through the Spirit.

The Vision of China & the Scroll

The burden for China was not new. For years, I had sensed the Spirit of the Lord drawing my heart toward the Chinese people. I would dream about them. I would weep for them. I would see cities and regions I'd never studied. My spirit would often pray in groanings I didn't understand, until God revealed the assignment. One night, I saw myself walking through the streets of China not with natural feet, but with the feet of obedience in the Spirit. I could feel the spiritual tension and sense the hunger of a people crying for truth.

That's when I knew: this nation is written in my scroll. The language, the stories, the food they weren't random interests. They were divine breadcrumbs leading me deeper into prophetic preparation. They were echoes of a mission already authored in eternity. *"You are My message,"* the Lord said. *"You are My Word in living form. The stage I am sending you to is My altar."*

From Watching to Walking

Being an "actress" in the story of God is not about performance. It's about surrender. It's about removing your name from the credits and allowing His name to shine in every scene. It means laying down your own ambitions and following the script He has already written even if it leads to places, you've never been. I have learned that true obedience often begins in the Spirit long before it manifests in the natural.

I have walked nations in my dreams. I have delivered prophetic messages for people and governments I've never met. I have seen cities before ever learning their names. And each time, the Holy Spirit whispers: *"You are not imagining these things. You are walking in them."*

Dressed for the Role

The Lord once told me in a moment of intense prayer: *"My covenant with you is sealed. Walk like My Bride."* Now, I no longer wonder what my place is. I am not lost in the crowd. I have been summoned to the King's chambers. I have been clothed with white robes and sealed with Heaven's ring. My role is not to impress but to obey. Not to seek applause, but to walk in divine authority. I now understand that everything I went through the losses, the isolation, the visions, the fire were all rehearsals.

They were all preparing me for the role that only I could walk out: a living epistle sent by God, an actress in the Story of the Lamb.

A Word to You, Reader

Perhaps you, too, have sensed strange passions rising for cultures, languages, or people you don't fully understand. Perhaps God has placed something in your heart that doesn't yet make sense. I urge you: don't dismiss it. You may think you are just watching. But Heaven may be preparing you to step into a scene already written. *"Before I formed you in the womb, I knew you. Before you were born, I set you apart."* — Jeremiah 1:5

You are not an extra in the background. You are not a bystander to revival. You are a living character in Heaven's greatest narrative, and the next scene is being written with your name on it.

Teaching

You Were Born for a Script Already Written

God is the Author of history, and He writes in scrolls, not in scripts we make up as we go. When He told Jeremiah, *"Before I formed you in the womb, I knew you"* — Jeremiah 1:5,

He revealed the eternal truth that every life is conceived first in the mind of God, not in the womb of a woman. Before time began, you were known. You were chosen. You were cast for a role in God's redemptive drama. Every divine calling begins in the Spirit. You do not need to physically stand in a place before Heaven sends your spirit ahead of you. In Scripture, Ezekiel was taken in the Spirit to the valley of dry bones (Ezekiel 37:1). John, on the isle of Patmos, was "in the Spirit on the Lord's Day" (Revelation 1:10) and saw the end of the age. These were not daydreams.

They were divine appointments outside of time and space. Heaven writes first. Earth walks it out later. When God begins to draw you to cultures, nations, languages, or people you have no natural connection to, it is often a sign that something in your scroll is being activated. The things that seem strange, random, or even trivial such as a love for a language or an unusual compassion for a region are often the Holy Spirit's way of awakening prophetic memory. Your life is not accidental. Your interests are not random. Your journey is not chaotic. *"In Your book they all were written, the days fashioned for me, when as yet there were none of them."* Psalm 139:16. The call to become an "actress in the story of God" is not a metaphor for ambition or performance.

It is the invitation to become a living epistle; a person whose life is read by others and reveals the glory of Christ (2 Corinthians 3:2–3). It is a call to surrender your personal script and embrace the greater scroll.

Reflections

Have You Been Watching What You're Meant to Walk?

- What passions, cultures, or nations has the Holy Spirit stirred your heart toward that don't make natural sense?
- Have you ever dismissed spiritual longings as "just a dream" or "just an interest"?
- Can you recall a time when you walked somewhere in the Spirit before seeing it in the natural?
- Are you ready to be written into God's unfolding story whether the stage is seen or unseen?

Sometimes, we are watching someone else's story and not realizing we are being prepared for our own.

When God stirs your affections or calls your attention to something repeatedly, don't ignore it. God often whispers before He sends.

Journal Prompt

Write to the Lord as the Divine Author. Begin with these words:

"Father, if I am part of a scene You have written, then I want to walk in it fully..." Ask the Lord to show you where you have been watching instead of walking. Write down any unusual spiritual interests you've had people, nations, languages, or burdens that won't leave your heart. Ask the Holy Spirit to confirm what is written in your scroll. Reflect on any dreams, visions, or moments of divine stirring you've experienced about a nation or people group. Let your journal become the rehearsal room where you agree with Heaven's script.

Prayer

Father, Eternal Author, you wrote my life before time began. You inscribed every scene, every page, and every purpose into Your divine scroll. Forgive me for the times I've clung to my own script, afraid of the unknown. Today, I surrender. I say yes to the stage You've designed for me. Even if I have never been there in the natural, I choose to walk there in the Spirit. Let every desire You placed in me be awakened for Your glory. Let every nation You've written on my heart become an altar where I carry Your presence. Clothe me in garments of readiness. Teach me to walk like Your Bride. I am not a background extra. I am a living word. Let my life bring glory to the Lamb who wrote my story with His blood. In Jesus' name, Amen.

Chapter 8

When God Breaks You to Multiply You

"And as they were eating, Jesus took bread, blessed and broke it, and gave it to the disciples and said, 'Take, eat; this is My body.'" — Matthew 26:26

He took the bread, He blessed it, He broke it, then He gave it. This is the divine order of God. Before He gives you to the world, He will first bless you, then break you, and only then can you be given. Many desire to be given, used mightily for the Kingdom, sent to nations, positioned in ministry, writing books, preaching with fire, but few are willing to be broken. Few understand that in the Kingdom of God, multiplication always follows breaking. I remember when the Lord led me into this revelation. I had prayed earnestly: *"Use me for Your glory, Lord!"*

And I meant it with all my heart. But I didn't yet understand what it would cost. He answered my prayer not with open doors, but with breaking.

The Breaking Comes After the Blessing

There was a season when everything in my life carried the fragrance of promise. I could feel the favour of God resting heavily upon me. His presence was near. Prophecies confirmed His call. Doors seemed to be opening, and then He broke me. Not out of anger, not out of rejection, but out of deep covenantal love. He broke the pride I didn't even know was lodged in my soul. He broke the need to be understood by man. He broke the desire to control the outcome of my obedience. He broke even the identity I had wrapped around my ministry. It wasn't just circumstances that broke me. It was God Himself. But in the breaking, I was not discarded. I was being prepared.

Broken Bread Feeds Many

Whatever God breaks, He intends to multiply. Like the five loaves and two fish, your little becomes much when placed in His hands and when broken. It is only in the breaking that bread becomes food for others. In this season of my life, I realized something painful yet beautiful: God was not trying to destroy me. He was trying to give me away. He was shaping me into a vessel that could carry His burden, His heart, and His tears for others. But He couldn't give me if I remained whole and self-contained. I had to be broken so that His life could flow through me. People don't need more performers or polished speakers. They need broken bread. They need poured-out wine. They need men and women who have died to self so that Christ may live fully through them.

Sealed in Blood & Brokenness

Jesus said, *"This is My body, broken for you."* He didn't just die for us. He let Himself be broken for us. That is His covenant, and now He calls us into the same covenant not just of His promises, but of His breaking and His giving. He whispered to me one night:

"Dorothea, I will take you; I will bless you; I will break you, and I will give you. This is not rejection. This is covenant."

I wept because in that moment, I finally understood. The brokenness I endured wasn't the end of my story it was the beginning of my multiplication.

Teaching

The Kingdom Pattern of Breaking

The pattern of taking, blessing, breaking, and giving is not a random detail in Scripture. It is a Kingdom principle:

1. **He Takes You** – This is divine selection (John 15:16).
2. **He Blesses You** – The impartation of grace and anointing.
3. **He Breaks You** – The removal of self-reliance (Galatians 2:20).
4. **He Gives You** – Only a broken vessel can pour out.

Why God Must Break You Before He Can Multiply You:

- Breaking removes self-glory (2 Corinthians 4:7).
- Breaking produces compassion.
- Breaking deepens dependence.
- Breaking enlarges capacity (Mark 14:3).

The Table of Covenant—breaking—is an invitation to deeper union.

Reflections

Have You Been Broken to Be Given?

1. Can you recognize seasons where God took you, blessed you, and then broke you?
2. Have you misinterpreted His breaking as rejection, rather than preparation for multiplication?
3. What areas of your life has God broken not to harm you but to give you to the world?

Journal Prompt

Write a personal letter to the Lord, reflecting on a time when you experienced deep breaking. In that letter, ask Him to reveal what He was preparing you for. How has that season shaped your calling or ministry?

Prayer

Jesus, thank You for Your broken body. Thank You for showing me that to be given, I must first be broken. I surrender to Your hands. Break what You must. Multiply what You will. And give me away to those who are hungry for You. Not my story, but Yours. Not my strength, but Your Spirit. Make me bread for the nations. Amen.

Chapter 9

The Broken Alabaster

"Truly I tell you," Jesus said, "wherever this gospel is preached throughout the world, what she has done will also be told, in memory of her." — Matthew 26:13

It was not a sermon, a prophecy, or even a miracle that caught the breath of Heaven that day in Bethany. It was the silent breaking of a vessel. A woman, unnamed in some gospels, walked into a room where men were seated around the Teacher, and she shattered her alabaster jar. The fragrance of worship filled the room, and judgment filled the hearts of men. But Jesus called it beautiful. I had read this story many times before, but I did not know what it meant to be the alabaster jar until I became it.

When Everything is Poured Out

There came a time in my life when everything that defined me was placed on the altar: my title, my marriage, my financial stability, my reputation, even my strength all of it broke open before the Lord. I wasn't standing in front of a crowd. I wasn't holding a microphone. I was on the floor, weeping. Nothing was left to give except myself. It was during one of those days alone, misunderstood, emptied, that I heard Him say:

"You are My alabaster box. I have allowed you to be broken before men, but it is for My fragrance to be released." The breaking did not come because I was disobedient. It came because He counted me worthy to be poured out. People often ask for the anointing, but they forget it flows from crushed olives.

They desire mantles but resist the mourning. They long for power but refuse the process. Yet the true fragrance of the Kingdom is not released until we are broken.

Teaching

The Altar of Costly Worship

Alabaster jars were not easily broken. They were sealed to preserve the perfume within. To pour it out meant it could never be gathered again. True worship costs something. And when it is poured out on Jesus, He never forgets it. He marks it as eternal. This woman didn't speak a word. Her act was her sermon. Her sacrifice was her voice. And Jesus said it would be remembered wherever the gospel is preached. Why? Because the gospel is not just about what we gain; it's about what we give. The breaking of the alabaster represents the place where your story and your surrender meet.

It is not about having it all together but about giving it all. Have you reached the place where your identity is no longer in the jar, but in the One who receives what was inside it?

Reflections

- What have you held back from the Lord because it felt too costly?
- Has God ever called you to pour something out without explanation?
- Can you see the beauty of your brokenness from Heaven's perspective?

Journal Prompt

Write about a time you felt like everything in your life was being poured out. What came out of that season? What fragrance did Heaven receive?

Prayer

Lord Jesus, you are worthy of all I have and all I am. Even when it hurts, even when I don't understand, I choose to pour out my life as worship. Let the fragrance of my surrender rise to You. Break me, if You must, so that You may be glorified in me. In Jesus' name, Amen.

Chapter 10

When What God Gave You Dies in your Hands

"By faith Abraham, when God tested him, offered Isaac as a sacrifice. He who had embraced the promises was about to sacrifice his one and only son." — Hebrews 11:17

There are deaths we can prepare for. Then there are deaths we never saw coming because the thing dying was promised by God Himself. What do you do when the very thing God gave you... dies in your hands? Not because of disobedience, but because of obedience. Not because you walked away, but because you kept walking forward. I have walked through this valley, and I tremble even now at its memory.

When the Promise Is Put on the Altar

Like Abraham, I was asked to lay something down something I loved something God had promised. It had a name. It had a face. It carried destiny.

But the voice of God came: *"Lay it down, offer it back to Me."* At first, I wrestled. *"Lord, you gave me this, you confirmed it, why would You take it now?"* Then I remembered: Isaac belonged to God before he belonged to Abraham. The promise was never mine to possess, only mine to steward. I bowed. I obeyed. I offered it back. And I watched as it died in my hands.

A Grief Few Understand

This is a unique kind of grief. When God asks for what He gave, few will understand your pain. They'll say, *"Wasn't its God who gave it to you?"* Yes. And that is what makes the surrender more piercing. How do you explain that the God who promised is the same God now asking for sacrifice? This death is sacred not because something ended, but because something deeper was born.

God, He Wanted Abraham's Heart not Isaac's Death

The altar was not about Isaac. It was about what Isaac represented:

- Fulfilled prophecy

- Answered prayer
- Future legacy

But when a promise becomes an idol, it must go back to the altar. Not because God is cruel, but because He is jealous for your full heart.

When the Promise Dies, the Promiser Stands

I have lived this. I have watched visions fade. I have seen relationships dissolve. I have buried assignments I thought would last forever. But in that grave, I found something greater: the God of the promise remained. When Isaac dies, Jehovah Jireh appears. When the dream ends, the Dream-Giver draws near. When what was visible fades, the Invisible One becomes all.

The Gift of the Grave

Here is what I've learned: Some promises must die so resurrection life can begin. You don't truly possess a promise until it's passed through death and back again. God never wastes a burial. If He allows you to bury something, it's because resurrection is in His plan. The death of the promise is the testing of your identity. Will you still be who He called you to be without the thing He gave?

Jesus – The Seed That Fell into the Ground

Jesus said:

"Unless a grain of wheat falls into the earth and dies, it remains alone. But if it dies, it produces much fruit." John 12:24

Even the greatest Promise of Heaven had to die. Jesus was not buried because He was defeated. He was buried to multiply. Likewise, your buried promise.

Teaching

Understanding the Death of The Promise in God's Kingdom

The "death of the promise" is one of the most misunderstood seasons in a believer's journey. It feels like loss, but in God's design, it is a sacred transition into greater fruitfulness.

- **The Altar Tests Ownership:** Abraham learned that Isaac was never truly his, he was God's. When God asks for what He gave you, it ensures your heart is anchored in the Giver, not the gift (Genesis 22:1–14).

- **Death Before Multiplication:** Nothing truly multiplies until it passes through death. Jesus, the ultimate Promise, died to bring many sons and daughters to glory (Hebrews 2:10).

-

- **Burial Is Not the End:** The grave is not God's full stop it's His comma. Lazarus lay in the tomb four days before Jesus called him forth (John 11:1–44). If it's in God's hands, it's never over.

- **Idols Are Often Good Things:** Sometimes the most dangerous idols are the blessings themselves. God tests our loyalty to see if we love Him more than these (John 21:15).

- **Resurrection Redefines the Promise:** When God raises something from the dead, it never looks the same. The resurrected Christ did not return to simply continue life as before; He entered glory.

Reflections

- Has God ever asked you to return something precious that He first gave to you? How did you respond?
- What "Isaac" in your life might need to go back to the altar so your heart stays fully His?
- How does knowing the Promiser remains give you hope when promises to seem to

die?

Journal Prompt

Write out the story of your "Isaac" the promise God gave you that has been tested or laid on the altar. Describe what it represented to you, how you felt when God asked for it, and what you discovered about His character through the process.

Prayer

Lord, you are the God who gives and the God who asks. Teach me to trust You with both the giving and the taking. When You place something in my hands, let me hold it loosely, knowing it belongs to You. If You ask for it back, help me to surrender without bitterness, knowing You are faithful. Resurrect what You will. Replace what You choose. But above all, keep my heart fully Yours. In Jesus' Name, Amen.

PART III

THE STORM & STILLNESS

Chapter 11

The Secret of the Wounded Watchman

"He was despised and rejected by men, a man of sorrows, and acquainted with grief..." — Isaiah 53:3

I never asked to become a watchman. I never prayed to see the things I see. I never wanted to feel the burden of nations or to weep for people I will never meet. But I was wounded into this calling. And the wound is the secret. One day in prayer, I cried out to God, asking Him why the visions always left me feeling bruised, and why the weight of what I saw lingered like a shadow over my soul. I didn't get an answer that day. Later, He showed me a vision: I was standing on a wall, looking out over a darkened land. I held a trumpet in my hand, but it was cracked. I looked down and saw the crack came from a wound in my chest. My heart had been pierced.

The Lord whispered, *"Your trumpet sounds through the wound. That is why it carries My sound."* This is the mystery of the wounded watchman. We don't blow the trumpet out of strength, but from the place where we were broken. The place where we died. Where we bled. Where we were rejected and misunderstood. That is where the sound comes from. It's not polished. It's not rehearsed. It's raw. It bleeds. It trembles. God uses our pain as His instrument. He doesn't remove the thorn; He anoints it. The wound becomes holy. And through that wounded place, the cry of intercession is born. When I walk through places of intense sorrow, rejection, or loss, I now recognize that He is stretching the capacity of my heart to feel what He feels. He is enlarging the wound so the sound may be deeper. The more crushed the vessel, the purer the oil.

This is the secret that few talk about. We want platforms, but we don't want pain. We want revelation, but we don't want suffering. But the secret of the true watchman is the wound.

Teaching

In the Bible, prophets and watchmen often bore the burden of the Word of the Lord.

- Ezekiel sat where the people sat for seven days, astonished and silent

(Ezekiel 3:15).
- Jeremiah wept rivers of tears for a people who would not listen.
- Isaiah spoke of the Suffering Servant, who bore wounds for others.

There is always a price to truly see and carry what Heaven reveals.

Watchmen are not simply those who warn; they are those who bleed. They stand between the porch and the altar (Joel 2:17), interceding for the people, weeping between Heaven and earth. The mark of a true watchman is not how loud they shout, but how deeply they feel. They know the secret of Christ's suffering and count it a joy to share in it. The calling of a watchman is a holy wound a burden that becomes prayer, a life poured out in hidden places.

Reflections

- Have you experienced God using your wounds for His glory?
- Do you feel the burden of intercession in a way that cannot be explained?
- How is the Lord teaching you to stand on the wall through pain.

Journal Prompt

Write about a time when your pain birthed prayer. How did God meet you in that place? What intercession came forth from that suffering?

Prayer

Lord, I give You, my wounds. Let them not be wasted. Anoint them with oil and let the sound of Heaven come through them. Make me a trumpet in Your hand, even if I am cracked. Let the pain I've walked through become a holy place where Your glory rests. I choose the hidden path of the watchman. I choose the wound. I choose You. Amen.

Chapter 12

Wisdom — A Friend Very, Very Old

It was 2020. I was praying and worshiping around 3:00 in the morning when suddenly, a brightness filled my bedroom. Colours of the rainbow reflected as different shades of light. I opened my eyes while still praying, sitting on my bed. Then I saw a man literally sitting on my bed. Even today, I can point to the very spot where he sat. He had curly hair as white as snow. Trembling, I asked God, *"Who is this man?"* The answer came:

"He is Wisdom, a friend very, very old."

I was overwhelmed by the holiness of that moment. It was not a distant vision; it was tangible. I could feel the weight of his presence.

He sat with authority and gentleness. His presence carried ancient understanding, a peace that spoke louder than words, and the brilliance of eternity. He didn't speak much; he didn't have to. His very being spoke volumes. That moment marked me for life. It was as if the timeless mind of God stepped into time to visit me not with noise or thunder, but with the calm and reverent weight of a Friend who has walked with God since before the foundation of the earth.

Teaching

The Spirit of Wisdom

The Spirit of Wisdom is not merely intellectual; He is a Person who flows from God's own being, one of the seven Spirits before His throne (Isaiah 11:2; Revelation 1:4). When Scripture says, *"Wisdom cries out in the streets,"* it is not just poetry. It is the living voice of an ancient companion of God's counsel (Proverbs 8:22–31). In Proverbs 8, Wisdom declares:

"The Lord possessed me at the beginning of His way, before His works of old. I have been established from everlasting... I was beside Him as a master craftsman." (Proverbs 8:22–30) This chapter reveals that Wisdom was present with God during creation, echoing the very language of eternity.

What I encountered that night was not just light; it was eternal counsel stepping into my room. The hair as white as snow reflects the imagery of the

Ancient of Days in Daniel 7:9, describing God Himself. It was as though what I saw was both a messenger and a manifestation a spiritual being carrying the fullness of Wisdom that originates from the very heart of God. This was not a dream. It was not sleep. It was real. A Friend very, very old.

Reflections

- Have you ever encountered Wisdom, not as a concept, but as a Person?
- Do you recognize the Spirit of Wisdom calling you to walk in insight, discernment, and divine timing?
- What would your life look like if you allowed Wisdom to sit beside you in every decision?

Journal Prompt

Write a letter to Wisdom as if writing to a deeply trusted and ancient Friend. Pour out your questions, confusions, and hopes, then listen. Ask: *"Wisdom, walk with me. Teach me the way of the Lord."*

Prayer

O Spirit of Wisdom, Friend of the Ancient of Days, walk with me. Sit on the bed of my soul and speak to me the counsel of the Lord. Let Your rainbow light floods every dark place in my understanding. You who were beside Him when the foundations were laid, help me build my life with divine strategy and holy reverence. I welcome You; I honour You, and I ask You to dwell in me. Amen.

Chapter 13

In The World but Not of the World

"Do not love the world or anything in the world. If anyone loves the world, love for the father is not in them." — 1 John 2:15

Living in this world as a believer is a constant tension. We are called to be salt and light, yet not to be shaped by the world's values, desires, or distractions. This chapter explores that sacred balance the call to engage the world without being swallowed by it. I remember the struggle of feeling both connected and isolated. I loved people, culture, and life, but I was constantly aware of a higher calling that demanded purity, holiness, and separation. I wanted to impact my generation, to relate to those around me, but never at the expense of compromising my walk with God.

The enemy tries to blur this line, tempting us to conform or retreat. Many believers wrestle with the pull of worldly approval, the desire to be liked, or the fear of being misunderstood. Yet God calls us to a higher standard, one that looks countercultural: to love the world without being of it.

Teaching

Walking the Sacred Tension

Being in the world but not of it is not about isolation or fear; it is about intentional engagement. Jesus Himself exemplified this balance. He lived among people, ate with sinners, and participated in daily life, yet His heart was never conformed to the world's priorities.

Key principles to help navigate this sacred tension:

1. **Set Your Values by Heaven's Standard** – Let God's Word define right and wrong, not trends or public opinion (Romans 12:2).
2. **Love People, Not Patterns of Sin** – You can be present in culture without embracing its vices. Influence without contamination.
3. **Guard Your Heart** – Be aware of what shapes your thoughts, emotions, and desires. The world's noise can dull your spiritual sensitivity.
4. **Purposeful Engagement** – Choose where and how you invest your

time. Be in the world with a mission, not a mirage.

Being separated does not mean being disconnected; it means being consecrated. The call is to stand firmly in God's truth while walking compassionately among humanity.

Reflections

- In what areas of your life are you conforming to the world without realizing it?
- How do you engage with people and culture while keeping your heart fully aligned with God?
- Are there relationships, trends, or desires you need to surrender to maintain spiritual purity?

Journal Prompt

Write about moments when you felt the tension between your faith and the world around you. How did you respond? Ask God to show you where He is calling you to stand firm, and how He wants you to engage without compromise.

Prayer

Father, help me to walk in the world without being shaped by it. Teach me to love people, culture, and life without losing my devotion to You. Guard my heart, align my desires with Your will, and give me wisdom to engage with purpose. May my life reflect Your light, standing out in truth, yet present with compassion. In Jesus' name, Amen.

Chapter 14

The Crown of Thorns

There are moments in life that leave a permanent imprint upon the soul moments where eternity invades time, and the presence of God becomes undeniably real. I remember such a moment vividly. It was not a dream; it was a divine visitation. I had just returned from a prayer walk, something I often did in those days to commune with the Lord. When I got back, I sat by the pool to pray a little longer before heading to bed. My husband was already asleep when I finally lay down. That's when He came.

The Lord Jesus appeared in my room. I did not see Him in full majesty, but in His agony. He wore the crown of thorns. His face was disfigured almost beyond recognition.

His head was bowed, and the thorns had pierced so deeply into His flesh that blood flowed in every direction. Tears of blood rolled down His cheeks, yet His eyes held no resentment only love. Painful, holy love. He looked at me with a sorrowful gaze that pierced my soul. Even now, when I am tempted to go astray, that look returns to convict me deeply. It reminds me of the price He paid what He endured to gain me. I began to weep uncontrollably. My heart could not contain the sight. This was not the glorified Christ; this was the rejected Lamb, the Man of Sorrows, despised and acquainted with grief.

When His eyes met mine, I felt the full weight of His suffering not just the physical torment, but the agony of betrayal, mockery, and abandonment. He had done nothing wrong. He had never sinned. He was perfect love, yet He wore the thorns that I deserved.

Then He spoke not with audible words, but in the deepest part of my spirit: *"Was My death in vain for you?"* It wasn't a rebuke; it was an invitation an invitation into the fellowship of His suffering. In that holy moment, something in me broke. I said yes through tears, through trembling, through the understanding that the path of surrender would not be easy.

The Call to Suffer with Christ

The crown of thorns was never just an instrument of mockery. It carries deep spiritual meaning it represents the curse, the pain, and the consequence of sin that entered the world after the fall. In Genesis 3:18, the ground was cursed to produce thorns and thistles, symbols of broken creation. When Jesus wore that crown, He took upon Himself the curse, becoming a curse for us (Galatians 3:13). He bore not only the pain of thorns piercing His brow, but the crushing weight of our sin, shame, and separation from God.

What man meant for humiliation, Heaven transformed into glory. The crown that mocked became the symbol of redemption. Paul expressed his longing in Philippians 3:10: *"That I may know Him, and the fellowship of His sufferings, being made conformable unto His death."* To truly know Christ, one must also share in His suffering. The path to resurrection power always passes through the garden of agony and the shadow of the cross. Suffering, when yielded to God, is not defeat it is sacred participation. It is the place where human pain meets divine love and where brokenness becomes a gateway to glory.

Reflections

Have you ever met Jesus in your pain not as the triumphant King, but as the suffering Savior? What does His crown of thorns mean to you? Is it a symbol of sacrifice, redemption, or divine love? And would you be willing to wear your own "crown of thorns" to embrace the suffering that purifies and draws you closer to Him? Suffering is not a curse for the believer; it is a communion a sacred union with Christ Himself.

Journal Prompt

Take a moment to write about a time when your pain mirrored His when your trials drew you nearer to the heart of Jesus. Reflect on what it meant to say "yes" to Him, even when it hurt. And if He were to ask you today, *"Will you wear this with Me?"* what would your answer be?

Prayer

Jesus, Son of God You wore the thorns, you bore the shame. You did not run from pain; You embraced it for me. Today, I kneel before You and say yes to Your will, yes to Your call, yes to carrying the cross with You. Let the image of Your suffering face never leave my heart. Let the thorns forever remind me of Your love. If I must suffer, let it be with You. If I must walk a narrow road, let it be beside You. I love You, Jesus not for what You give, but for who You are.

Chapter 15

Daughters Of the Secret Place

"But you, when you pray, go into your room, and when you have shut your door, pray to your Father who is in the secret place; and your Father who sees in secret will reward you openly."
— Matthew 6:6

There is a sacred intimacy that is born in the secret place the hidden chamber of prayer, worship, and communion with God. It is here that the daughters of the Most High are formed, strengthened, and prepared for their divine destiny. The secret place becomes a refuge from the chaos, noise, and demands of the world. It is a spiritual sanctuary where the weary soul can lay down its burdens and meet the Lover of our souls in purity and peace. For me, the secret place has often been both a battlefield and a sanctuary a place of wrestling and surrender.

There were seasons when I fled to that sacred chamber because the pressures outside were unbearable. Yet within that hidden refuge, the presence of God overshadowed every fear, doubt, and confusion.

The Power of the Secret Place

The secret place is not merely a physical room it is a divine reality that transcends space and time. It is where the veil between Heaven and earth grows thin, and God's glory descends to commune with His children.

In this hidden place:

- The weary find rest.
- The broken find healing.
- The called find clarity.

History is filled with women who carried the mantle of revival, leadership, and intercession because of their hidden lives with God. Their public power was birthed in private devotion.

Consider Anna the Prophetess (Luke 2:36–38), a woman who worshiped and fasted day and night in the temple. Her quiet faithfulness positioned her to witness and proclaim the arrival of the Messiah.

Formed As Daughters

Daughters of the secret place are marked by perseverance, faithfulness, and deep intimacy with God. Their power is hidden but potent. They do not seek applause or public acclaim they live for an audience of One. In a world that prizes visibility, performance, and instant gratification, the secret place calls us to a different rhythm one of patience, obedience, and trust. It is here that God cultivates the fruit of the Spirit, shapes character and refines purpose. It is here that prophetic words are whispered, divine strategies are revealed, and supernatural strength is imparted for the journey ahead.

The Discipline of the Secret Place

Entering the secret place requires discipline and consistency. It is easy to become distracted or discouraged, yet consistency is the key to intimacy. Even when you don't "feel" like praying, showing up strengthens your spirit and honours God. Sacrifice is also necessary. Sometimes, entering the secret place means giving up comfort, sleep, or entertainment to commune with the father. Expectation fuels faith come before Him expecting to hear, to see, and to be transformed.

Practical Encouragement

- Create a dedicated time and space for your secret place encounters.
- Guard this time zealously against distractions and interruptions.
- Keep a journal to record what God reveals in those moments.
- Connect with other daughters who value the secret place for mutual encouragement and accountability.

Teaching

- The secret place cultivates intimacy and transformation.
- God rewards those who seek Him sincerely and persistently.
- Spiritual authority flows from the hidden place into public ministry.
- Consistent prayer and worship build resilience for the battles ahead.

- The enemy fiercely attacks the secret place because it births destiny.

Reflections

- How often do you retreat to your secret place with God?
- What distractions or excuses keep you from deeper intimacy?
- How has your time in the secret place shaped your faith and calling?
- What practical steps can you take to guard and grow your secret place life?

Journal Prompt

Reflect on your journey in the secret place. Write about a powerful encounter, a breakthrough, or a lesson learned there. How has that hidden intimacy prepared you for what lies ahead?

Prayer

Father, thank You for the secret place the holy chamber where I can meet You face to face. Teach me to prioritize this sacred time above all else. Help me to remain faithful even when it's difficult or inconvenient. Strengthen me to persevere in prayer, in worship, and in waiting upon You. Let the intimacy I cultivate in secret overflow into every area of my life. Use me, your daughter, to reveal Your glory and bring Your kingdom to earth. **In Jesus' name, Amen.**

PART IV

REDEMPTION OF TIME & HOLINESS

Chapter 16

Hidden in the Shadow of His Hand

"He made my mouth like a sharpened sword; in the shadow of His hand, He hid me; He made me into a polished arrow and concealed me in His quiver."
— Isaiah 49:2

There was a season in my life when I couldn't understand why everything around me seemed to close in. I wasn't living in sin. I wasn't in rebellion. I had obeyed the voice of the Lord, yet doors began to shut. People I thought would stand with me grew distant. Invitations stopped coming. Prophetic words that once flowed so freely became few and far between. My voice felt silenced. I remember crying out to God, *"Lord, why are You hiding me?"* Over time, I learned that it wasn't punishment. It wasn't rejection. It was protection divine concealment.

I was being hidden in the shadow of His hand. Looking back now, I see that season differently. It wasn't the absence of God it was His presence covering me like a mantle. I was in the shadow, but I wasn't alone. I was being forged in a furnace no one could see. The anointing was deepening. My motives were being purified. My identity was being redefined by God Himself.

Why God Hides You

- **To build the inner man:** Before God uses you publicly, He must establish you privately. The hidden place is where your foundation is dug deep where character, prayer life, and endurance are forged in the dark.
- **To break all dependencies:** We often lean on people, platforms, and props more than we realize. When God hides you, He strips these away, so your trust rests solely in Him.

Biblical Examples of Hiddenness

The Scriptures are filled with examples of men and women God chose to hide before revealing them:

- **Moses** spent forty years in the wilderness tending sheep before

WHEN GOD ASKS FOR EVERYTHING

returning to Egypt as a deliverer.

- **David** was anointed king but spent years hiding in caves from Saul.
- **Joseph** was imprisoned in a dungeon long before he ruled in Pharaoh's palace.
- **Jesus** Himself lived thirty years in obscurity before his public ministry began.

Each of these were **hidden but not forgotten, delayed but not denied.**

What Happens in the Hidden Place?

- **Deep intimacy is formed:** Without the spotlight, you learn to lean into the whispers of God. The hidden place becomes a sacred sanctuary of communion.
- **The oil of the secret place increases:** Anointing is not manufactured it is cultivated. In isolation, the oil flows. The private altar becomes holy ground.
- **You are re-identified by God:** In hiddenness, God gives you a new name that no one else knows. It's no longer about titles, but identity who you are *in Him.*

When God Places You in the Shadow

Sometimes we mistake silence for absence. But the silence of God is often the clearest evidence of His nearness working deeply, shaping silently, loving fiercely. The cave is not the grave. It is a place of transition, not death.

You are not **buried** you are **being planted.**

And in due season, you will rise.

Reflections

- Have you ever felt God hiding you in a season when you expected exposure?
- In what ways is God refining your motives in private?

- Are there dependencies He's asking you to release?
- What truths has God whispered to you in the hidden place?
- How can you learn to embrace the shadow instead of resisting it?

Prayer

Lord, you see me when no one else does. You know my heart. Refine my motives, break false dependencies, and build my inner life. Teach me to love the shadow if it means I am close to You. Let me not despise the season of obscurity but find my identity in You alone hidden yet held; concealed yet called. In the shadow of Your hand, I am safe. **In Jesus' Name, Amen.**

Chapter 17

The Place: Where Secrets Are Shared

There are places in God that cannot be accessed in public. They are not loud, not advertised, and not impressive to the natural eye. These are the **secret places** the realms of whispers, where God shares His deepest thoughts with those He trusts. It is not the outer court, nor even the Holy Place it is the **Holy of Holies**, that inner chamber where the veil is drawn and His voice is unfiltered. It was during one of the darkest seasons of my life that I discovered this sacred dimension. I had been stripped of many things' relationships, support, and even the understanding of those I loved. I felt abandoned, unseen, and misunderstood.

Yet it was in that place of utter aloneness that I began to encounter God in a way I never had before. I remember lying on the floor one day not praying, not interceding, simply being still. And then, suddenly, I heard Him whisper, *"I have been waiting for you here."* His voice wasn't loud, but it carried a divine weight. The atmosphere shifted, and I knew I had entered the **secret place**. It wasn't a physical location; it was a realm in the Spirit a place that only **hunger and surrender** can take you. From that day forward, He began to entrust me with things that shook me to the core revelations about nations, dreams warning of coming dangers, and visitations of angels. The spirit of prophecy increased with fire, but so did the cost. For once you are trusted with divine secrets, you must live as one **set apart**.

Teaching

The Mystery of the Secret Place

Psalm 91:1 declares, *"He who dwells in the secret place of the Most High shall abide under the shadow of the Almighty."*

This is more than a promise of protection it is a **pathway to intimacy**. The secret place is where God hides those, He desires to reveal Himself to.

Moses had to climb the mountain.

Elijah had to hide in the cave.

Jesus often withdrew to solitary places to commune with the Father.

What they found there was not mere information it was **revelation**. They didn't just receive messages from God; they encountered **God Himself**. Secrets are not given to the curious they are reserved for those in **covenant**. God does not reveal mysteries to those chasing signs and wonders, but to those who seek His heart.

That's why Proverbs 25:2 says, *"It is the glory of God to conceal a matter, but the glory of kings to search out a matter."* In the secret place, God tests your heart. He trains your ear to hear beyond the noise. He molds the character of the prophet before releasing the message. This place is not glamorous it's hidden. But once you've tasted it, nothing else will ever satisfy you again.

Reflections

- Have you discovered the secret place in your walk with God?
- Are you allowing Him to entrust you with His secrets, or are you too hurried for intimacy?
- Do you desire the public platform more than the private presence?

Journal Prompt

Write about a time when you felt God drawing you into deeper intimacy. What were the circumstances? What was the cost? What did He reveal to you in that moment?

Prayer

Father, draw me into the secret place where Your voice becomes my sustenance. Strip away the noise, the pride, and the distractions that keep me from intimacy with You. I want to dwell where You dwell, abide where You abide, and know You beyond the veil. Trust me with Your secrets, Lord not for status, but for surrender. In Jesus' name, Amen.

Chapter 18

When God Asks for Your Isaac

Encounter

There are moments in every believer's journey that test the deepest places of trust and surrender. For me, that moment came like a sharp sword piercing through my spirit when God asked me for my Isaac. It wasn't a physical child it was a promise, a dream, a hope I had nurtured and cherished. It represented everything I held dear. I remember that day vividly. I was kneeling in prayer, tears streaming freely, when the gentle yet firm voice of the Lord spoke to my heart: "Remove your husband from the place you have placed him in your heart, and I, the Lord, will find a place where he fits in you."

My heart stopped. Fear, confusion, and sorrow crashed over me like waves. My Isaac was not just a person—it was a symbol of God's covenant, of His blessing. To give up Isaac meant surrendering the future I had imagined, the legacy I had hoped to build. Not long after that encounter, the weight of surrender became tangible. I lost my marriage, the home I had known, and everything I had built. My world seemed to collapse around me. The pain was deep, and the loneliness was suffocating. Yet, even in the midst of such loss, God's voice remained steady inviting me to trust Him beyond the breaking. It was not a command meant to wound, but an invitation to intimacy. He was teaching me that true worship is found in obedience, not comfort, in surrender, not possession. In that sacred moment, I understood Abraham's test. I saw the altar, the wood, the knife raised in trembling obedience. And I realized the test was never about losing Isaac.

It was about trusting God's heart beyond understanding. It was about saying, *"Not my will, but Yours be done."*

Teaching

The story of Abraham and Isaac stands as one of Scripture's most profound lessons on faith and surrender. God's request was not just about obedience it was about trusting the promise even in the face of pain. Isaac represented the fulfilment of God's covenant the seed through which nations would be blessed. To offer Isaac meant placing everything precious into God's hands, even when the act seemed to contradict the promise. Hebrews 11:17–19 reminds us that Abraham obeyed *"by faith,"* believing that God could raise Isaac from the dead if necessary. When God asks for your Isaac, it may not be a child. It may be a dream, a relationship, a calling, a ministry, or even your reputation. It may be that one thing you believe defines your purpose or future.

But here's the truth God never asks for your Isaac to take life away. He asks so He can resurrect it in His way and His timing. The altar is not the end it's the beginning of transformation. What feels like loss becomes the seed of new life. Your surrender becomes a living testimony of God's faithfulness and a revelation of His resurrection power.

Reflections

◇ What is your Isaac the thing most precious that God may be asking you to surrender?

◇ How do you respond when God asks for something that feels impossible to give?

◇ Are you willing to trust His provision even when the promise seems delayed or lost?

◇ How have your own seasons of loss shaped your faith and understanding of God's character?

Journal Prompt

Reflect on a time when you faced a painful surrender. How did God meet you in that season? What did you learn about His faithfulness, and how did the experience transform your understanding of trust? Write down how that moment reshaped your walk with Him.

Prayer

Father God, you are the giver of every good and perfect gift. You have blessed me beyond measure, yet You call me to surrender what I hold most dear. Teach me to trust You with my Isaac. Help me to obey even when I do not understand. Strengthen my faith to believe in Your resurrection power. Let my surrender rise as a fragrant offering before You. In Jesus' name, Amen.

Chapter 19

The Weeping Altar

"I looked for someone among them who would build up the wall and stand before Me in the gap on behalf of the land so I would not have to destroy it, but I found no one."
— Ezekiel 22:30

When Christ Weeps in You

I will not call it a vision but since that day Christ appeared to me in the way He did, something inside me was never the same again. That encounter marked me forever with a compassion that no language can describe. There were no flashes of light or thundering voices this time—only a deep sorrow that pierced my spirit, a holy burden that clearly did not come from me.

It was Him. The One who had appeared to me before. The One whose eyes hold eternity, and whose wounds still bleed mercy.

From that day onward, I began to weep in prayer—not for myself, but for nations. For cities I have never walked through. For people I have never met. For souls who may never experience His love unless someone intercedes. I wept because I saw His heart, and I felt His pain. I realized that God's greatest desire is not judgment—it is salvation.

I understood then that the Spirit of God lives in every human being, that He fashioned each one with divine purpose. And when that revelation truly reaches your spirit, you cannot pray casually anymore. You weep. You groan. You feel His anguish for the lost. You become one with His cry.

Christ weeps in us. The Cross is no longer something distant—it becomes something you carry. His tears begin to fall through your eyes. His intercession begins to echo through your voice.

Teaching: The Intercession of Christ in Us

When the presence of Christ takes residence in your life, prayer changes its nature. You no longer pray from emotion; you begin to pray from His burden.

Intercession is not simply asking—it is the groaning of God through a yielded vessel.

"Likewise, the Spirit also helps our infirmities... but the Spirit Himself makes intercession for us with groanings which cannot be uttered." — Romans 8:26

There is a sacred depth in prayer where words end, and tears begin. It is in that silent travail that God's heartbeat becomes audible.

I remember one day while driving to fetch my children from school, the Lord allowed me to see His heart. It appeared before my spiritual eyes as if it were being torn into pieces. Then I heard Him say,

"This is how My heart is. Every time My children sin against Me, it is as though My heart is being cut to pieces."

I broke down in tears. I could see myself in one of those cuts—in His pain, in His mercy. That day, I realized something profound: God feels. He bleeds with us, and He longs for us.

When you truly carry the Cross, you begin to carry souls. You feel what He feels. You cry without knowing why. You travail for nations you've never seen. You whisper the names of places that you only know by the Spirit. That is what it means to stand in the gap.

Jesus is the High Priest who "ever lives to make intercession for us" (Hebrews 7:25). And when He dwells in you, His intercession continues through you. You become His voice, His tears,

His cry, His heartbeat moving toward the lost. This is not just ministry—it is a holy burning.

Reflection Questions: Has the Cry of Christ Entered Your Heart?

◊ *Have you ever felt the burden of God's heart for someone else?*

◊ *Are you willing to carry a nation in prayer, even if no one ever sees it?*

◊ *Can you set aside your own desires long enough to feel His longing for souls?*

God is not seeking eloquence—He is searching for yielded hearts that say, "Here I am, Lord, weeping with You."

Journal Prompt

Write a heartfelt prayer for a nation, people group, or city that the Holy Spirit has placed on your heart. Don't filter it let your tears speak. Allow the Spirit to intercede through you.

A Sacred Altar Call: The Heart Song of the Lamb

Right now, the Lamb who was slain stands knocking on the door of many hearts. He whispers,

"Will you carry My burden for the nations? Will you cry with Me until My lost ones return home?"

This is not a call to a title or position—it is a call to become a womb for revival.

If this cry burns within you, lift your heart before God and say:

"Here I am, Lord. Birth in me the tears of intercession. Let my life become an altar. Let my heart become a nation's cry."

Final Cry of Intercession

Oh Lord of the Harvest, we weep with You. We stand before You on behalf of the nations, the tribes, the tongues, and the souls who have not yet heard Your name.

We cry for the children, the mothers, the prisoners, and the broken-hearted. We cry for the prodigals and the rebellious.

Let Your Spirit sweep across the earth again. Let revival visit dry lands and cold hearts. Let the Cross be lifted high. Let the fire fall upon ordinary men and women. Let salvation invade the streets, homes, prisons, and palaces.

We cry not for ourselves, but for the glory of the Lamb to fill the earth.
Here we are, Lord—let the weeping altar rise from within us.

Until You come.
Until all have heard.
Until the nations worship the Lamb.
Amen.

Chapter 20

Where the Anointing Is Born

There is an altar where oil is made not by the shout, but by the crushing; where mantles are not worn for status, but weep with the fragrance of Gethsemane. I found myself there once in the place where everything that made sense was stripped away. My job was gone, my health was fragile, and relationships I had trusted were stretched to breaking point. One night, kneeling on the cold floor, I whispered into the silence, *"Lord, when will the pain end?"*

It was there in that suffocating stillness that the oil of my calling began to flow. In a dream, I saw a jar in the Potter's hand. I was that jar. But He did not crush me in anger; He pressed me gently on the wheel, reshaping what was broken.

The cracks I once despised became the very windows through which His light shone. That season didn't destroy me it refined me. It was then I understood: the weight of the anointing cannot rest on an unbroken vessel. Gethsemane became my classroom. I watched again as Jesus, in the Garden of Crushing, bowed His humanity before His Father's will. *"Not My will, but Yours be done."* In that surrender, heaven's power began to pour through Him.

The Garden was the threshold of glory a place where pain birthed power, and obedience unlocked destiny. The oil pressed in silence would later anoint the feet that walked in victory. I thought I knew surrender before that night, but the crushing demanded a deeper death a more dangerous obedience that whispered,

"Even if You slay me, yet will I trust you. "And from that place, came the oil. Not for platform, but for purpose. Not for title, but for testimony. Not for applause, but for authority. And the price of that oil was *everything.*

The Crucible of the Spirit

Crushing is not cruelty it is divine crafting. Every anointed life carries the fingerprint of pain. Just as olives must be crushed to release their oil, so must the believer pass through pressure to release the glory within. The crushing produces oil the Spirit's power, presence, and purity. Without it, there is only potential, not potency. The crushing refines the vessel purging pride, teaching dependence, molding character. The crushing prepares the heart making it pliable, teachable, and completely surrendered. And the crushing releases new anointing a fragrance that changes atmospheres and breaks yokes.

So, if you find yourself in the press, remember: Gethsemane comes before glory. The hand that crushes you is the same hand that anoints you.

Reflections

- What areas of your life feel pressed or broken right now?
- Can you discern God's fingerprints in your crushing?
- What might He be refining or preparing in you through this pain?
- Are you willing to trust Him even when the oil flows through tears?

Journal Prompt

Write about a season that felt unbearable yet birthed something new in you. What fragrance of grace emerged from your breaking? How did you see God's hand in what once felt like loss?

Prayer

Lord, I come before You with open hands and a trembling heart. Crush what must be crushed until only You remain. Break my pride, purify my desires, and let the oil of Your presence flow freely through me. May every wound release worship, and every tear birth testimony. Let my life carry the fragrance of Your crushing a living offering to the glory of Your name.

In Jesus' name, Amen.

PART IV

THE PRODIGAL JOURNEY

Chapter 21

Living The Script of Heaven

I always knew my life was not ordinary. But it wasn't until the Lord said to me, *"You are an actress in the story I am writing,"* that everything finally clicked. The scenes of my life both bitter and beautiful were not disconnected chaos, but part of a divine screenplay authored by the hand of God Himself. The day He showed me China was unlike any other. I wasn't physically there, yet my spirit was caught up in a vivid prophetic vision. I found myself standing on what looked like a grand movie set. The atmosphere was charged, sacred, and alive as though something eternal was being filmed. There were lights, cameras, and movement, but I wasn't performing for men. Heaven was watching.

I saw my name written in Chinese characters, and though I had never studied the language, I understood it perfectly. Then the Lord said, *"Your role in this nation is already written. Step into the scene."* My heart trembled. I saw streets I had never walked, faces I had never met, yet a deep love consumed me. The Father was directing a story far greater than I could comprehend and I wasn't just in the audience. I was part of the cast. A vessel. An actress in His unfolding masterpiece.

This calling was never about fame or platform. It was about surrender. Every act in this story demanded obedience even when obedience meant losing everything I once held dear. Some scenes were filled with tears, suffering, and the silence of waiting. Others overflowed with revelation, joy, and glory. But all were necessary.

There were moments when I wanted to walk off set times I longed to rewrite the script. Yet the Director never lost sight of the ending. He held the storyboard. He knew every scene before I stepped into it. Every delay, every crushing, every divine encounter was perfectly timed. One night, weeping over my calling and the cost of it, I cried out, "Father, am I forgotten?" He replied so tenderly, *"Dorothea, you are on My screen. The world may not see you yet, but Heaven is watching your every move. You are exactly where I placed you."*

This chapter of China is one of those sacred assignments. I do not yet know the fullness of what it means, but I know I'm being prepared. The scenes are unfolding. Heaven's script is still being played out in me. And so, I remain in position in costume with my heart yielded, saying, *"Yes, Lord. Let Your will be done. I am Yours to direct."*

Teaching

The Divine Narrative

We often forget that our lives are not a series of random events, but part of a divine narrative authored by God. Romans 8:28 reminds us, *"All things work together for good to those who love God, to those who are the called according to His purpose."* We are not spectators in the Kingdom we are participants. Even when the scenes we walk through feel confusing or painful, the Master Director is still in control. He writes roles into our lives that we do not always understand in the moment.

Like Esther, prepared in obscurity for a moment before kings. Like Joseph, whose betrayal became the bridge to the palace. Each of us is uniquely positioned in the Kingdom's storyline. When God told me I was an actress in His story, He wasn't diminishing my identity He was defining it.

In Greek, the word *hypokrites* (used for actors in ancient plays) appears in Scripture as a warning against religious performance. But in the Spirit, the Lord whispers something different: *"You are not performing for men you are fulfilling a heavenly script. And your audience is not the earth. It is Heaven.* "To understand our place in God's storyline, we must embrace seasons of preparation, obscurity, and obedience. You may not yet understand your role, but Heaven has cast you for a reason. Your *yes* matters.

Reflections

- What has God revealed to you about your unique role in His Kingdom story?
- Are there areas where you've resisted the script because of fear, pain, or uncertainty?
- How do you respond when it feels like no one is watching your obedience but God?

Journal Prompt

Write a letter to the Lord as if you are accepting the role He has written for you. Surrender your fears, your need for control, and your desire to know the next scene. Invite Him to direct your life afresh.

Prayer

Father, thank You for writing me into Your divine story.

Even when I don't understand the scene, help me trust the Director. I yield to Your purpose and surrender my script. Let my life be a vessel for Your glory. Whether hidden or seen, let every act of obedience please You. Teach me to stay in position, with my heart and eyes fixed on You. In Jesus' name, Amen.

Chapter 22

My Garden of Gethsemane

"Let us fix our eyes on Jesus, the author and finisher of our faith, who for the joy set before Him endured the Cross, scorning its shame, and sat down at the right hand of the throne of God." — **Hebrews 12:2**

There comes a point in every believer's journey when God asks for something deeper something costlier.

For me, that moment came when the Lord stripped away everything, I had ever called mine: my marriage, the home I had built, and the dreams I held so close to my heart. It was as if everything I loved had been laid bare on the altar of surrender, and I was left holding only one thing the Cross. I had prayed for the glory of God. I had longed to carry His presence in a way that would transform lives, nations, and generations. Yet I did not know that the path to that glory would first lead through **Gethsemane**.

There were days I wept like Jesus in the garden, pleading, *"Father, take this cup from me."* But beneath every cry of pain was a deeper surrender: *"Nevertheless, not my will, but Yours be done."* I did not realize it then, but the Cross was making way for the Fire, and the Fire was preparing me for the Glory.

The Cross: A Place of Death & Love

The Cross is more than a moment in salvation history. It is the daily road of those who follow Jesus. It is the place where God asks for what we cling to not because He is cruel, but because He is holy.

The Cross demands everything:

- Your rights.
- Your reputation.
- Your self-preservation.
- Even your desire to be understood.

It was on the Cross that Jesus bore the shame, the silence, and the rejection and yet, He still loved. The Cross is where we are emptied of self so that Christ may be fully formed in us. Many desire the power of resurrection, but few are willing to embrace the death that precedes it.

The Furnace of Refinement

If the Cross is the altar, then the Fire is the process. God does not bring us through death to leave us lifeless He sends the Fire to refine. The Fire of God is not meant for destruction but for purification. Like gold tested in the furnace, our faith must be tried so that it may be found pure, beautiful, and strong. I remember nights when I felt like I was burning alive through pain, betrayal, and loss. Yet, in those very flames, I saw Jesus more clearly than ever before. He walked with me, just as He walked with the three Hebrew boys in the fiery furnace.

And when I came out, not even the smell of smoke clung to me. The Fire took away everything that could not enter the next season it burned off pride, exposed mixture, and consumed false ambition. What remained was one thing: a holy hunger for God.

The Fruit of Surrendered Lives

Oh, the Glory that follows the crushing! It is not a mist that fills a service or a goosebump in worship.

It is the abiding presence of the Holy One resting upon a soul that has died, been refined, and now lives for one purpose to reveal Christ. The Glory does not visit where the Cross is rejected. The Glory does not remain where the Fire is resisted. But to the one who says *yes* truly *yes* to the dealings of God, the Glory comes. This is the Glory I have known in my journey:

- In the peace that guards my heart even when I have nothing.
- In the fire of the Spirit that ignites when I preach the Word.
- In the tangible presence that fills the room when I worship in secret.
- In the holy weight that falls when I pray for nations.

The Glory rests where the Cross has been embraced and the Fire has done its work.

Jesus: Our Pattern & Prize

When Jesus sweat drops of blood in Gethsemane, He wasn't weak He was surrendered. His humanity cried in anguish, but His divinity bowed in obedience.

- His Cross became our redemption.
- His Fire became our empowerment.
- His Glory became our inheritance.

And now, we are invited to walk the same journey from Cross, to Fire, to Glory.

Reflections

- What areas of your life is the Lord asking you to surrender to the Cross?
- Have you mistaken the Fire for abandonment, when it was really His refining love?
- Are you yearning for the Glory of God and what has He asked you to lay down first?
- Can you trace how God has used suffering to prepare you for something greater?

Journal Prompt

Write about your personal *Gethsemane moment* a time when God asked for everything. What did it cost you? What did He show you in that place of surrender? How is the Fire preparing you for His Glory?

Prayer

Abba Father, I yield again. I lay down my desires, my plans, my comfort, and my control. I choose the Cross, no matter how painful. I say yes to the Fire, no matter how long. And I hunger for Your Glory not to be seen, but that You may be seen in me. Let my life carry the fragrance of Christ. Let me be trusted with the weight of Your Glory not for ministry or fame, but because I have been found faithful in the hidden place. Burn away all that hinders love. Raise in me a life that reflects Jesus crucified, refined, and glorified in resurrection power. In Jesus' name, Amen.

PART VI

THE COVENANT BRIDE

Chapter 23

When He Is in the Storm

There are storms we rebuke. There are storms we endure. And then there are storms that *carry Him*. I have known all three. There was a season when I was praying, fasting, and weeping waiting for God to stop the winds. But instead of the storm ceasing, it intensified. The more I prayed, the louder the winds howled against me. I expected divine intervention. I expected the waters to still and the clouds to part. But instead... **Jesus slept.** I remember whispering in the dark, "Jesus, do You see what's happening to me? Do You care that I am perishing?" And silence met me not the silence of absence, but the silence of a Sovereign God who was in the boat, though He had not yet stood to speak.

It was then that I began to understand a different side of Him the Christ who is still Sovereign, even when He is silent. The One who trusts you enough to walk through a storm without panicking, because He already knows the outcome. His silence was not neglect; it was divine trust. It was as though Heaven was saying, *"You know Me by now. You've seen Me still storms. But now, I want you to know Me in the storm."*

This was the storm that taught me not to be afraid of the waves, but to discern **the Presence in the boat.** He was there. And He was sleeping not because He was indifferent, but because the storm was never a threat to Him. He wasn't panicked, and He didn't need to be. He *was* peace itself. The fiercest storm is not always the one outside it's the one inside. It's the voice of fear, abandonment, and anxiety that whispers, *"He's not coming."* But it's also the place where faith grows teeth where peace is no longer a feeling, but a Person.

I learned to surrender to the storm He was in, not to fight it. I stopped praying for survival and began asking for surrender. I stopped resisting and started resting in Him. Storms like these strip us. They remove false securities. They remove the need for control. They sanctify. And most importantly they reveal *Him*.

Teaching

The Presence of Christ During Chaos

In **Mark 4:35–41**, the disciples find themselves in a life-threatening storm while Jesus sleeps on a cushion in the boat. They panic but He is perfectly at rest. When they finally wake Him, He rebukes the wind but also their unbelief. This passage reveals that the peace we need is not found in calmer circumstances, but in the *Person* of Christ. He *is* peace. And where He is, peace is possible—even when the wind rages.

His sleep was not ignorance it was trust. He knew they would cross over. And He knew the storm had no authority to cancel what He had already declared: *"Let us go over to the other side."* There is also a deeper revelation here: sometimes the storm is not sent to destroy you, but to **reveal the authority within you.** When He arose and rebuked the wind, the disciples were in awe: *"Even the wind and the sea obey Him!"*

Could it be that your storm is a setup for a new revelation of His dominion? In Gethsemane, Jesus Himself faced an internal storm: *"My soul is overwhelmed to the point of death."* Yet He did not run. He surrendered. He stayed in the storm not because He enjoyed the pain, but because He trusted the Father. Some storms are not meant to be stopped. Some storms are meant to be stewarded.

Reflections

- Have you been through a storm where Jesus felt silent or absent?
- What did you expect Him to do—and what did He do?
- Did you find Him *in* the storm... or only *after* it passed?

Journal Prompt

Write about a season when everything around you were shaking and you thought God had forgotten you. Can you now look back and see that He was there even if silent? What did you learn about His **presence** versus His **intervention**?

Prayer

Jesus, I don't always understand why You stay silent when storms rage. But I choose to believe that You are in the boat. Teach me to rest as You do to trust in Your Word more than I trust in the waves. Help me to surrender, even when You don't still the wind. Let me find peace not in *what You do,* but in *who You are.*

In **Jesus' name, Amen.**

Chapter 24

Be Still & Know

There are moments in the journey when you've fasted, prayed, obeyed, cried, and surrendered and still, the mountain remains unmoved. The Red Sea doesn't part. The enemy still breathes threats on every side. The promise feels delayed. And heaven seems quiet. It is in these moments that the Spirit whispers: **"Stand."**

I remember a season when I had done all I knew to do. I had obeyed the last instruction. I had emptied myself in prayer. I had wept until there were no more tears. And still, nothing changed. It was a wilderness between word and fulfilment, and it broke me. One day, while reading Ephesians 6, the words leapt from the page: "...and having done all, to stand." (Ephesians 6:13). I paused. I realized God wasn't asking me to do *more*.

He was asking me to *trust* more. To stand. To stop striving and let His strength be made perfect in my weakness. Standing is not passive it's an act of war. It is refusing to retreat when your soul wants to quit. It is anchoring your feet in truth when lies scream louder. It is choosing to believe what God said, even when you cannot see it. There's a stillness that is not silence. It is sacred. It is the stillness of Exodus 14:14: "The Lord will fight for you; you need only to be still." That phrase *"be still"* is not inactivity it is surrender. It is the warrior's posture of resting in the Commander's presence. I came to the end of myself in that season. I stopped trying to fix what was beyond my control. I stopped trying to open doors God had shut. I put down my sword and knelt in worship. And slowly, heaven began to move. Doors opened without striving. Miracles came without manipulation. The storm passed without my hand on the wheel. I learned that the fiercest faith is sometimes not in *shouting* but in *standing*.

Teaching

The Power of Standing Still

Standing is a faith posture. It is part of the armour of God in **Ephesians 6**. Paul repeats the word *"stand"* several times:

- "Put on the whole armour of God, that you may be able to stand against the schemes of the devil."
- "Take up the whole armour of God, that you may be able to withstand in the evil day, and having done all, to stand firm."

This reveals something powerful: there is **warfare in standing.** It is a resistance to the enemy a refusal to bow to fear or compromise.

There's also a divine stillness commanded in Scripture. **Psalm 46:10** says, "Be still, and know that I am God." The Hebrew word for *"be still"* (*raphah*) means *to let go, to release, to cease striving.* When the Israelites were trapped between Pharaoh and the Red Sea, Moses declared: "Stand firm, and you will see the deliverance the Lord will bring you today." (Exodus 14:13) God parted the sea not while they fought but while they **stood still.**

Reflections

- Have you reached the end of your strength in a situation?
- What would it look like for you to *stand* in this season rather than strive?
- Can you trust God to fight for you while you remain still in worship?
-

Journal Prompt

Write about a season when you did everything you could, but nothing seemed to move. How did you respond? Can you now see how God was working even in the stillness?

Prayer

Lord, when I have done all and nothing changes, teach me to stand. Help me rest in You when the storm rages. Teach me the strength of surrender and the power of stillness. I lay down my striving. I anchor myself in You. **Fight for me, Lord.** I will stand, worship, and wait. In **Jesus' name, Amen.**

Chapter 25

Redeeming the Time

"See then that you walk circumspectly, not as fools but as wise, redeeming the time, because the days are evil."
— *Ephesians 5:15–16*

I once saw time as something to be managed, stretched, or even wasted when I didn't feel the weight of purpose. But then something shifted. The Lord began to open my eyes to the spiritual significance of time not as a human calendar, but as a **divine currency**. There are moments in life when you feel eternity breathing on you. Heaven opens, and you see the clock of God ticking not in minutes and hours, but in **seasons and urgency**. I began to realize that certain doors are open only for a while, certain graces are tied to moments, and certain assignments carry divine deadlines.

The Lord began to speak to me about *redeeming the time* to **buy back** what had been lost, delayed, or neglected. This wasn't just about productivity; it was about prophetic awareness. The hour was late. The harvest was ripe. And many were still asleep. In prayer, I saw a vision of a great clock suspended over the earth. It was the father's timepiece. Angels moved swiftly; scrolls were being dispatched. I heard the words:

"Tell them to redeem the time for many are wasting the moments I've anointed for obedience."

In that same season, the Holy Spirit began awakening me at specific hours of the night. It was as if **time itself was being sanctified**. Every interruption carried an assignment. I realized that when time is surrendered to God, it becomes holy it becomes a seed that yields eternal fruit.

This chapter in my life brought **repentance**. I thought of the years I had spent doing things God never asked me to do. I repented for delayed obedience, for small compromises, and for distractions disguised as good opportunities. God wasn't punishing me He was calling me back into alignment. He was restoring the years the locust had eaten.

If you're reading this and you feel like time has slipped through your fingers, know this: **God can redeem it.** He is the Alpha and the Omega. He can compress time. He can multiply grace. He can accelerate your steps to catch up with His purpose. But first, you must awaken.

Redeeming the time means:

- Saying no to what doesn't align with His will.
- Being fully present where He places you.
- Living with the awareness that your life is a vapor — precious, fleeting, and full of purpose.
- Understanding that the battle over your time is a battle over your destiny.

The urgency of the hour is not about fear — it's about **focus**. Heaven is moving swiftly. Kingdom purposes are being fulfilled. God is still looking for those who will say, "Yes, Lord, in this moment. I won't delay again."

Teaching

Walking In God's Timing

God's time is not always our time. He is not moved by calendars, but by **Kairos** *appointed times.* **Chronos** time is sequential: Monday, Tuesday, January, February.

Kairos time is divine a pregnant moment when God determines that something eternal must take place. To *redeem the time* is to live not only wisely, but **prophetically**. You begin to sense what the Spirit is doing in the moment, and you respond with urgency and faith. Jesus often said, *"My hour has not yet come."* He walked in perfect timing. He never rushed. He never lagged. He moved in rhythm with the Father.

Now, in these last days, we are called to do the same.

Reflections

- Where have you lost time due to disobedience or distraction?
- What areas of your life do you sense the Holy Spirit calling you to redeem?
- Are you living in alignment with God's divine seasons?

Journal Prompt

Write a prayer of repentance and realignment. Ask the Lord to reveal how you can redeem the time in this season and step fully into your prophetic assignments.

Prayer

Father, awaken me to the urgency of the hour.

I repent for every way I've wasted the time You've entrusted to me. Thank You for Your mercy that You redeem, restore, and realign. Teach me to number my days, that I may gain a heart of wisdom. Let my time become worship. Let my days reflect Your design. In **Jesus' name, Amen.**

Chapter 26

Kept for His Use

"Therefore, I urge you, brothers and sisters, in view of God's mercy, to offer your bodies as a living sacrifice, holy and pleasing to God this is your true and proper worship."— Romans 12:1

I went through a divorce after twenty-six years of marriage. It was the painful death of something I had built with my whole heart a tearing apart of the soul, a silence louder than screams, and a loneliness deeper than any ocean I had ever known. I had stood by a covenant I believed in. I fought for a home I thought would last. But one day, it stood empty. And in the stillness of that grief, I heard Him not with condemnation or judgment, but with a whisper, gentle and clear:

"Keep your body holy for My use." Those words wrapped themselves around my spirit. It wasn't a command from a harsh master, but a request from the One who loved me most. He wasn't asking for perfection; He was asking for **consecration**. I have walked this journey now for seven years seven years of quiet consecration of trusting when I did not understand. There have been tears, moments when the flesh cried out for companionship, and times when I questioned whether this path was still necessary. Yet, every time, His Spirit reminded me *why*: because I am His wholly, completely, without reservation. This chapter of my life is not marked by shame or failure. It is marked by **obedience, purity, and surrender**. I have become His altar. And I know He is writing a new story with my life one that will speak hope and healing to many who have walked through the pain of broken covenant.

Teaching

The Holy Offering of a Consecrated Body

After seasons of loss or betrayal, it can be tempting to seek comfort in the arms of another or to medicate the pain through relationships. But often, God calls His daughters to a higher path a **consecrated walk**, a journey of sanctified solitude. Not because He wants to deny us love, but because He wants to **rebuild us in holiness**. The body is not just flesh and bone it is a **temple**. When God says, *"Keep your body holy,"* He is inviting us into the same covenant of purity the Nazarites walked in (Numbers 6) and the same devotion Paul encouraged the early believers to uphold (1 Corinthians 6:19–20). This kind of consecration is **prophetic**. It becomes a living sermon a testimony that in a world where sexuality is used to define worth, God raises women whose worth is defined not by who touched them, but by **Who dwells within them**.

Reflections

- Have you ever felt God call you to a season of consecration? How did you respond?
- In what ways have you struggled with loneliness or the loss of covenant? How did God meet you in that pain?
- How does your current lifestyle reflect holiness unto the Lord?
- What would it mean for you to present your body as a "living sacrifice" in your own context?

Journal Prompt

Write a letter to the Lord from the place of your consecration. Tell Him what it has cost you, what you've learned, and what beauty and burden have come from this obedience. Then ask Him what fruit He is birthing through your surrender.

Prayer

Father, thank You for calling me to Yourself even in the midst of pain. Thank You for not allowing my story to end in divorce, but to continue as a testimony of consecrated love. I offer You my body, my emotions, my future everything. Keep me holy, Lord. Keep me surrendered. I choose You over everything else.

Let my obedience open the way for healing in many others. In **Jesus' name, Amen.**

PART VII

PROPHETIC WHISPERS

Prophetic Journal Entry #6

The Altar of Worship
  Date: May 2024 – Botswana

In May 2024, during a time of consecration in Botswana, the Lord met me in a way that marked my spirit deeply. I wasn't in the front or holding any visible role that day; I was simply there to worship. Yet, during the gathering, a prophetess a woman I had never met before approached me with a word from the Lord. She said, *"You have established an altar of worship before the Lord."*

Those words pierced me. For years, I had lifted my hands in worship in the quiet of my room, in public gatherings, and in moments hidden from all eyes but his. It was never about performance or recognition. It was always an offering a silent cry of love and surrender rising from my spirit to His throne.

Then the Holy Spirit spoke clearly: *"When you do that, I release My Presence where you are."* At that moment, everything connected. I realized why atmospheres would shift when I worshiped, why His nearness would wrap around me like fire, and why visions and revelations would come in those moments of pure adoration. That word in Botswana wasn't random it was a divine confirmation that heaven had seen the secret altar I had built before the Lord over the years.

Now I understand: my hands lifted in worship are not mere gestures; they are priestly acts offerings upon the altar of a surrendered life. Worship is the place where heaven meets earth, and my life itself has become that altar.

Prophetic Journal Entry

Title: The Covenant Bride: No Marriage
Date: Unknown Year

Encounter Description

I remember the voice of the Lord Jesus coming to me clear, sovereign, and filled with divine purpose. It wasn't a suggestion; it was a covenantal call. He said, *"No marriage. Enter the Covenant Bride. When people look at you, they should see My Bride."* Those words pierced my soul. They were not a denial of love, but an invitation into a higher one a sacred separation unto Him. I didn't understand the full meaning then, but I knew this moment would mark my life forever. There was no trace of sorrow in His voice only glory, peace, and purpose. This call was not about loneliness; it was about belonging wholly to Him. About walking as a living prophecy.

In that moment, I understood: the Lamb had claimed me not merely for ministry, but for Himself. When He said, *"When people look at you, they should see My Bride,"* I knew that my life would become a mirror a living testimony of devotion, purity, and surrender. The fragrance of Gethsemane, the life of the Cross, and the fire of resurrection would all flow through an unmarried vessel chosen to carry His name without veil. Sometimes I still ask,

"Lord, what did I do to deserve this kind of love?" But I realize it is not deserved. It is covenant. It is purpose. It is Him choosing me, and me saying yes.

Reflections

◊ Could it be that our journey is not about what we gain, but about what we become?

◊ Could it be that to walk unmarried is not a loss, but a bridal calling to become a visible sign of the bride awaiting her Bridegroom?

Seal of the Spirit

"And I looked, and I saw the bride prepared for her Husband, clothed in white, without spot or wrinkle... And the Spirit and the Bride say, 'Come.'"
— Revelation 21:2; 22:17

Prophetic Journal Entry #5

Title: *The Covenant Bride: The Marriage of the Lamb*
Dates: 2007 – 6 July 2025

Encounter Description

In 2007, the Lord began to lead me on a sacred journey. He said, *"Write the book about marriage."* I remember responding through tears, *"Lord, my own marriage has so many cracks I can hardly breathe. How can I write about something so broken?"*

It felt impossible. My earthly marriage was marked by pain, disappointment, and silent struggle. Yet, even during that brokenness, the Lord was pointing to something far deeper than the union between man and woman.

Years later, in 2023, His voice came again this time with unmistakable clarity: *"Enter into the marriage covenant."* But this was not an earthly covenant. The Lord said, *"This is the Marriage of the Lamb and the Church."* Then came a weighty revelation that shook me to the core: *"If believers cannot understand this marriage, they will struggle to understand My marriage."*

On the 6th of July 2025, during a time of deep worship, His presence descended upon me again thick, holy, and tender. I heard His voice clearly: *"Enter the covenant and honour it."* In that moment, I knew I was standing on holy ground. I finally understood He was never just speaking about a natural marriage. He was inviting me, and the Body of Christ, into the mystery of divine union: to live as His covenant Bride. To embody the purity, faithfulness, and consecration of the Church waiting for her Bridegroom.

He said to me once more, *"When people look at you, they should see My Bride."* This entry belongs in this journal not because I fully comprehend it, but because the Holy Spirit asked that it be written. There is a reason. There is a witness. There is a call, and I have chosen to obey.

Prophetic Journal Entry

Title: *Vision Of the Silver Bowl: A Warning to the Shepherds*
   Recorded By: *Dorothea Telephone Mokgadi*
   Date Of Vision: *2007*
   Fulfilment and Release: *2022–2025*

Vision Description

I saw a vision of a silver bowl being carried, filled with a black substance. The Lord spoke clearly: *"Tell the pastors they are feeding My people poison."* The warning was sharp, clear, and terrifying. The silver bowl itself was beautiful radiant and polished on the outside, but its contents were dark, thick, and defiled. I could literally smell sulphuric acid rising from it. I knew immediately that it represented sermons and teachings that looked refined, godly, and polished externally, yet were full of compromise, self-exaltation, and spiritual contamination.

I trembled. In tears, I responded, *"But how will I tell them, if I myself do not know?"* I felt unworthy, untrained, and too young to carry such a weighty word. That same year, 2007, I tried to enrol in Bible College out of obedience and desperation to know the Word, but the doors did not open. It was only fifteen years later, in 2022, that the Lord allowed me to begin formal study at World Harvest Theological College. The same vision returned, even more intense, and I realized that it had been waiting for its appointed time.

Message And Revelation

This vision is not one of condemnation, but of urgent mercy. The Lord is calling His shepherds back to the pure food of the Word the untainted gospel of Christ. The cloud of witnesses is watching. The 24 elders are bowing. Heaven is not silent. The Holy Spirit is being poured out with power, but He will not endorse poison from the pulpit.

This vision, now written in this book, is part of the scroll I was asked to live. It belongs here because:

- The Cross demands purity.
- The Fire burns away mixture.
- The Glory will not rest on defilement

Final Chapter

When Nothing Is Left but God

There comes a point in every believer's journey when the noise fades, striving ends, and all that remains is God. It is the sacred place beyond human ambition, beyond ministry, beyond promises and dreams—the place where all things are surrendered, and the soul whispers, *"Lord, you alone are enough."* When God asks for everything, He is not taking from us to wound us He is purifying love itself. The hand that breaks is the same hand that builds; the fire that consumes is the same flame that crowns. In those silent, unexplainable seasons when the heavens seem closed and every effort falls apart, Heaven is preparing the altar where glory will descend.

I have learned that obedience is not measured by what we do for God but by what we are willing to lay down before Him. When you have truly surrendered, there is no fear left to bargain with, no pride left to defend, no dream left to control. The cross removes everything that once defined you so that Christ alone becomes your definition. In my own journey, there came a day when I realized I had nothing left to offer but a heart still burning for Him. Titles meant nothing, strength was gone, and even my understanding of calling had been reduced to ashes. Yet, in that emptiness, I discovered something eternal. His presence. It was not the fire of ministry or the anointing for nations, but the quiet nearness of the Holy One who walks in the gardens of broken hearts. This is the mystery of divine exchange: when God strips a life bare, He does so to reveal Himself as the only treasure worth keeping. The world may call it loss, but Heaven calls it glory.

Every tear, every hidden pain, every unanswered prayer becomes the oil that lights the flame of His dwelling within us. You cannot see the glory of resurrection until you have embraced the silence of the tomb. The cross is not the end it is the threshold. Beyond the last surrender lies a beauty no language can capture. It is the place where obedience meets glory, where death gives birth to divine life, where all that remains is Christ living through you. When nothing is left but God, that is when everything begins again not as before, but as Heaven intended from the foundation of the world. In that holy aftermath, you no longer chase destiny; destiny flows out of you. You no longer seek power; power quietly rests upon you. You no longer try to be seen; you have become His hidden vessel, through whom His glory is revealed. The true measure of fulfilment is not in what we accomplish, but in how much of Christ is formed in us.

When He finally becomes your only ambition, you realize that every wilderness, every crushing, every unanswered question was part of the journey that led you back to the centre the Person of Jesus Himself. So, when He asks for everything, do not fear. When He takes you through the fire, do not resist. When He empties you, do not despair. Because in the end, when nothing is left but God, the glory beyond the cross rises in you like the morning sun. This is the mystery of the surrendered life. This is the story Heaven writes upon those who say *"yes"* when it costs everything. And this is where I now rest: in the hands of the Author who finishes what He begins until all that is left is Christ in me, the hope of glory.

Conclusion

The Heartbeat of the Journey

As I pen these final words, I look back on every chapter and see not a book, but a pilgrimage a sacred unfolding of grace. From the earliest whisperings of God's voice to the fiery seasons of the Cross, every moment has been a thread woven into the tapestry of His divine purpose for my life.

I have come to understand that knowing God is not a race to be won, but a journey to be lived one of unveiling, pruning, and discovery. There were times I thought I was lost, yet I was being led. There were moments I felt forsaken, yet I was being formed. Writing this book has shown me the contours of my own prodigal path the striving, the silence, the breaking, and finally, the stillness that births surrender.

Every wilderness, every fire, every unanswered prayer has been a classroom of the Spirit. And through it all, I have found that God does not waste a single moment. What once felt like delay was divine design. What seemed like loss was redirection. What appeared silent was sanctification.

A Prodigal Daughter

I realize now that I have been a prodigal daughter not in rebellion, but in misunderstanding the mysterious ways of God. I wandered through seasons of striving, questioning, and attempting to make sense of His purpose through human logic. Like the prodigal son, I was not lost in sin but lost in comprehension. I tried to measure divine timing with earthly clocks, to define heavenly purpose through human sight. Yet, even in my wandering, His love never left me. His hand never stopped guiding me.

To be prodigal is to experience the humility of realizing that understanding God is not about control it's about trust. It is to learn that His ways are higher, His timing perfect, and His plans beyond our reasoning. It is sacred, because it brings us home to His heart. And so, I return not empty but overflowing. Overflowing with the truth that God's love is eternal, His process perfect, and His purpose unstoppable. To the one reading this who feels lost, confused, or far from God: you are not forgotten. You are not behind. Even in your wandering, God is weaving redemption through every moment. He is teaching you, molding you, and preparing you to understand Him more deeply than ever before.

Teaching

Understanding The Prodigal Path

- **Misunderstanding God's Timing:** We often rush His process, assuming we know the better way. Yet, every delay is a divine appointment teaching us patience and trust.
- **Relying on Our Own Strength:** Spiritual prodigals strive in their own power to fulfil what only the Spirit can complete. Surrender is the only key to alignment.
- **Learning Through Humility:** Wandering seasons humble us. They strip us of pride and prepare us for intimacy with God.
- **Discovering God's Faithfulness:** Even when we misunderstand or fall short, God's love remains. He redeems every detour and uses it to draw us closer to Himself.

Reflections

- Where in your journey have you been "prodigal" in understanding God's ways?
- What lessons has God taught you in seasons of confusion or delay?
- How can you embrace His timing and trust His leading more fully today?
- In what ways has God shown Himself faithful, even when you couldn't see it?

Journal Prompts

1. Write about a season where you felt spiritually lost or misunderstood God's plan. How did He eventually bring clarity?
2. Identify areas where you may still be trying to "force" outcomes. How can you release them to God's control?
3. List three ways God's faithfulness carried you during your wandering.
4. Describe how it feels to walk forward now not in striving, but in trust and understanding.

DOROTHEA MOKGADI

Prayer

Father,

I confess the times I have been a prodigal when I misunderstood Your ways, tried to control Your plans, or wandered in impatience. Yet, through it all, you never left me. Thank You for guiding me even in the wilderness, for shaping me through the silence, and for loving me into surrender. Teach me to trust You're timing. Teach me to walk in step with Your Spirit.

Teach me to see even my wandering as sacred ground. Today, I return not as a stranger, but as a daughter, whole and restored. Let my life forever echo the heartbeat of this journey: *to know You, to love You, and to walk humbly in Your will.* In **Jesus' Name, Amen.**

Closing Note

May this book not only tell my story but become a lamp for every reader walking their own road of faith. May it lead you into a deeper understanding of God's ways His timing, His refining, His silent mercies. May it awaken trust where fear once lived, humility where pride once stood, and courage where weariness tried to settle. And may you remember always: even in the prodigal seasons, when understanding fades and silence surrounds you, God's love has never departed. His wisdom is still guiding. His hand is still writing.Walk faithfully, beloved for every step, even the uncertain ones, is part of His divine story unfolding through you.

ABOUT THE AUTHOR

Dorothea Telephone Mokgadi is an ordained prophetic voice, writer, and vessel of divine communication, called to reveal the heart of God to the nations. Born in Legonyane Village, Northwest Province, South Africa, Dorothea's life has been marked by profound encounters with the voice and presence of God from a young age. Her unique middle name, *"Telephone,"* was divinely given to signify unbroken communication between Heaven and Earth a living expression of her prophetic mandate. She walks in intimate obedience to the Lord, carrying a message of surrender, holiness, and restoration. Her guiding verse, *"Be holy, for I am holy"* (1 Peter 1:16), resonates through her writings and every step of her spiritual journey. Through seasons of crushing, refining, and divine fire, Dorothea has come to embody the message of her book a call for believers to yield wholly to God's transforming love. She holds a Diploma in Theology and is a final-year student pursuing a Bachelor of Theology at World Harvest Theological College, where she is mentored by Dr. Pika.

His Christ-centred approach, *"Let the Bible speak for itself,"* has deeply shaped her understanding of expository preaching and spiritual integrity. Dorothea's prophetic assignments extend beyond borders, including recurring visions and spiritual visitations concerning China and other nations. She serves the Body of Christ through prophetic teaching, intercession, and mentorship, with a burning desire to prepare the Bride of Christ for the coming King. Her ministry and writings flow from a deep well of intimacy with God, weaving personal testimony with revelation to inspire believers into deeper communion with the Holy Spirit. She continues to pour out her life as a living scroll an active participant in the unfolding story of God.

THE END

Don't miss out!

Visit the website below and you can sign up to receive emails whenever Dorothea Mokgadi publishes a new book. There's no charge and no obligation.

https://books2read.com/r/B-A-OCUXE-DETEI

BOOKS 2 READ

Connecting independent readers to independent writers.

About the Author

ABOUT THE AUTHOR

Dorothea Telephone Mokgadi is an ordained prophetic voice, writer, and vessel of divine communication, called to reveal the heart of God to the nations. Born in Legonyane Village, Northwest Province, South Africa, Dorothea's life has been marked by profound encounters with the voice and presence of God from a young age. Her unique middle name, *"Telephone,"* was divinely given to signify unbroken communication between Heaven and Earth a living expression of her prophetic mandate. She walks in intimate obedience to the Lord, carrying a message of surrender, holiness, and restoration. Her guiding verse, *"Be holy, for I am holy"* (1 Peter 1:16), resonates through her writings and every step of her spiritual journey. Through seasons of crushing, refining, and divine fire, Dorothea has come to embody the message of her book a call for believers to yield wholly to God's transforming love. She holds a Diploma in Theology and is a final-year student pursuing a Bachelor of Theology at World Harvest Theological College, where she is mentored by Dr. Pika.

His Christ-centred approach, *"Let the Bible speak for itself,"* has deeply shaped her understanding of expository preaching and spiritual integrity. Dorothea's prophetic assignments extend beyond borders, including recurring visions and spiritual visitations concerning China and other nations. She serves the Body of Christ through prophetic teaching, intercession, and mentorship, with a burning desire to prepare the Bride of Christ for the coming King. Her ministry and writings flow from a deep well of intimacy with God, weaving personal testimony with revelation to inspire believers into deeper communion with the Holy Spirit. She continues to pour out her life as a living scroll an active participant in the unfolding story of God.